Temple of the Twelve
Experiential Journal

Temple of the Twelve
Experiential Journal

Esmerelda Little Flame
and
David J. Babulski, Ed.D

Illustrations
David J. Babulski, Ed.D

An Imprint of Andborough Publishing, LLC

New Gaia Press
www.NewGaiaPress.com
Colorado Springs, Colorado 80922
USA

Temple of the Twelve: Experiential Journal
Copyright© 2008 Gemma Dubaldo and David J. Babulski, Ed.D.
First New Gaia Press trade paperback printing August 2008
ISBN - 13   978-0-9774181-7-6

Library of Congress Control Number: 2001087321

All Rights Reserved: Except for fair use in book reviews, no part of this publication may be reproduced or transmitted in any form or by any means, electronic or mechanical, including photocopying, recording, or any information storage and retrieval system or technologies now known or later developed or invented, without permission in writing from the publisher.

This is a work of fiction. Names, characters, places and incidents are either the product of the author's imagination or are used fictitiously, and any resemblance to actual persons, living or dead, business establishments, events or locales is entirely coincidental.

New Gaia Press is an imprint of Andborough Publishing, LLC
www.Andborough.com

Printed in the United States of America

Dedication

This book is dedicated to every dear reader who seeks to bring the colors into their life.

— Esmerelda Little Flame

Dedicated to every reader who dares to dream of worlds yet to be explored, and who secretly wishes to make the colors an integral part of their life.

— David Babulski

Acknowledgements

David, Priest of Blue, the circle in which we dedicated ourselves to the Twelve lives into infinity. You have taken my story to a whole new level, and made it soar.

— Esmerelda Little Flame

Contents

Acknowledgements	7
Section One	13
The Experiential Journal	13
The Depth of Black	21
The Caring of Pink	24
The Magic of Silver	28
The Wisdom of Blue	31
The Passion of Red and the Life of Green	35
The Passion of Red and the Life of Green Continued	39
The Glory of Orange	43
The Sacredness of Purple	46
The Security of Brown	50
The Rebirth of White	54
The Power of Gold	57
The Hope of Yellow	61
Section Two	69
Using this Journal with Children	69
Self-Portrait at the End of Your Journey	75
Achievement Chart	77
Map of Chroinia: The World of the Twelve	78
The Authors	81

Temple of the Twelve
Experiential Journal

Section One
The Experiential Journal

In *Temple of the Twelve, Volume 1: Novice of Colors*, Esmerelda Little Flame has written a coming of age story that also addresses many of the spiritual questions and issues that we all deal with as we live our own lives. This experiential journal is designed to assist the reader in growing right along with the heroine of the story, Caroline "Little Bird" as she grows into young adulthood and answers many of the same spiritual questions we all ask as we seek the Divine.

A discussion of what color is, from both a scientific and spiritual point of view, and how color affects all of us as human beings, opens the journal. The next chapter discusses the world of the Temple of the Twelve and how it is similar and different from our own world. The preparatory chapter is closed out with a discussion of how color is used by the author to represent the various aspects of Deity as they impact Little Bird, and by extension all of us as we search for our place in the world and our relationship to Divinity.

A series of twelve chapters follows. Each chapter is keyed to a corresponding chapter in the novel. Through the use of questions and guided exercises, the reader is encouraged to quest for the Divine right along with Little Bird. It is important to note that there are no right or wrong answers to the questions. Instead, the reader is encouraged to examine his or her own life in light of the quest that Caroline is undergoing.

In the novel, as Caroline completes each task or challenge assigned to her by an aspect of Divinity represented by a color, she is awarded a colored feather to symbolize her achievement. Likewise, as the reader completes each section, they color in a feather symbol on a page provided at the back of the journal.

When the reader has completed all the sections of this experiential journal, they are encouraged to record their observations on how they have changed as a result of their quest along with Caroline. A special section is provided at the end of the journal for this purpose. At the end of this book there is also a section with helpful hints for parents who wish to do these exercises with their children. If you are ready, let's begin the adventure along with Caroline. But first, a discussion of color and how it is used is in order.

Temple of the Twelve

WHAT IS COLOR? – A SCIENTIFIC POINT OF VIEW

In its most basic form, we can think of color as a psychological response to a physiological stimulus in the retina of the human eye by electromagnetic radiation in the 400 to 700 Terahertz frequency band. Radiation in this region of the electromagnetic spectrum is called "Visible Light" as we humans convert the perception of this energy to the sensations of light and dark and color. As humans we perceive electromagnetic radiation at a frequency of 700 Terahertz as the color Violet and a frequency of 400 Terahertz as the color Red. The other colors of the visible spectrum are between these two frequencies. The diagram shown in figure 1 illustrates the position of "visible light" in the overall electromagnetic spectrum.

gion with electrons that are part of the atoms that make up the surface of the object. The specific electron energy levels of the atoms that make up the surface will determine which frequencies of visible light are absorbed and which are reflected from the surface of the object. For example, an object that appears to us as Red does so because the frequencies of visible light that we perceive as Green and Blue are absorbed and those frequencies of visible light that we perceive as Red are reflected to our eyes. We can say then that the human perception of color in the world that we live in is the result of how we as humans interpret the selective absorption and reflection of electromagnetic waves in the 400 to 750 Terahertz frequency band. Scientists most often refer to visible light in terms of wavelength rather than frequency.

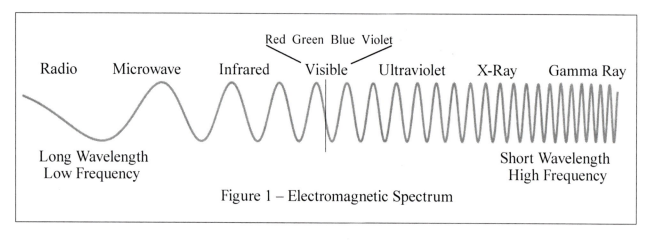

Figure 1 – Electromagnetic Spectrum

Electromagnetic radiation is produced by the transfer of energy by electrons within the smallest particle of matter, the atom. We all live in a sea of electromagnetic radiation both natural and artificial. This radiation is composed of oscillating electric and magnetic fields at right angles to each other and propagating through space. This combination of oscillating fields is called an "electromagnetic wave". A diagram of the relationship between oscillating electric and magnetic fields is shown in figure 2.

Color is not an inherent property of an object, but rather results from the interaction of electromagnetic waves in the 400 to 700 Terahertz re-

Wavelength is a measurement of the distance between adjacent peaks in the electromagnetic wave. Wavelength is used because of the large

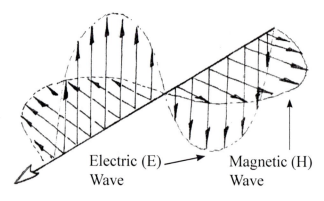

Figure 2 – Electric and Magnetic Fields

number of zeros when using frequency notation that makes calculations cumbersome. For example: The color red is a frequency of 400 Terahertz or 400,000,000,000,000 hertz (That is a lot of zeros!) and is equal to a wavelength of 750 nanometers. This is often abbreviated as "nm". The color violet is a frequency of 700 Terahertz and is equal to a wavelength of 430 nm. We will refer to the wavelength of visible light for the remainder of this discussion.

WHAT IS COLOR? – A SPIRITUAL POINT OF VIEW

It is important to remember that the notion of "Color" is based on human perception of electromagnetic radiation in the 400 to 700 nanometer portion of the electromagnetic spectrum. Without this human perception, this electromagnetic radiation remains just that – undifferentiated electromagnetic radiation. Color is the physiological perception of specific wavelengths of electromagnetic radiation. How each person interprets this perception depends on culture, education and individual psychology. For our purposes in this section we will define psychology as a spiritual belief system. As an example, let us examine the color red. In the western magical traditions, red symbolizes passion, strength, lust energy, anger, action, projection and courage to name just a few. However, in Eastern thought, the color red has different meanings such as prosperity, good luck, love, and good fortune. Examples from some of the major religious systems of the world will show how the same perceptions of color can have very different meanings depending on personal cultural bias.

In the Christian religious tradition, colors have the generalized meanings listed below:

Yellow: Symbol of light and purity. It speaks of youth, happiness, the harvest, hospitality, love and benevolence.

Orange: Symbol of endurance and strength, orange is the color of fire and flame. It is the red of passion tempered by the yellow of wisdom.

Green: Symbolic of the breaking of shackles, freedom from bondage. In the Christian context green represents bountifulness, hope and the victory of life over death.

Red: Symbolic of action, fire, charity, spiritual awakening. In Christian symbolism, red denotes the Holy Spirit and the color of Pentecost.

Black: Symbolic of the absolute, constancy, eternity. Black may also mean death, fear and ignorance.

Brown: In the Christian tradition brown is symbolic of the earth, humility and God's connection with the commonplace.

Blue: This color signifies life-giving air and often is symbolic for hope or health. Some use blue as a color for the season of Advent.

White: Symbolizes purity, virginity, innocence and birth. In the Christian tradition white is the color of Christmas and Easter.

Purple: This color speaks of fasting, faith, patience and trust. It is the color of penance, Advent and Lent.

In the Buddhist spiritual tradition, colors are defined differently as listed below:

White: White is thought to have a very cold quality, as in snow, or an extremely hot quality, such a burning metal. Either can be life threatening and can be a reminder of death and the end of things. Thus, the Goddess Tara, in her form that grants longevity to worshippers, is depicted as white-hued (White Tara).

Red: In Buddhist thought red is the color of powerful rituals and deeds. It is the color of passion, transmuted to discriminating wisdom.

Yellow: Yellow is the color closest to daylight. It has the highest symbolic value in Buddhism through its link with saffron robes of monks.

Green: Green symbolizes the qualities of balance and harmony. Green also denotes youthful vigor and activity. As a result, the Green Tara is always shown as a young girl having a mischievous and playful nature.

These are but a few examples of how we as human beings define the spiritual aspects of color. Because each person experiences the perception of color differently, there are as many individual definitions of the spiritual aspects of color as there are people, as opposed to the very precise scientific definition of color. The notion of color is a uniquely human interaction. Throughout the history of humankind, the perception of color has had a profound influence on the human condition. Temple of the Twelve explores this influence of color on the human condition in a way that transcends all specific religious traditions.

THE WORLD OF TEMPLE OF THE TWELVE

The world of the Temple of the Twelve is an Earth-like planet orbiting in second position around a Class "G" dwarf yellow star very similar to our own Sun. Six interconnected continents and several small island chains separated by large areas of ocean make up the surface of the planet. Each of the continents has a mix of topography ranging from majestic mountain peaks, lush forests, vast sandy beaches, and dry desert areas. Each continent is home to a pair of the twelve colors. In the native language this world is called Chroinia, which means "land of many colors" in the native language. The largest of the continental landmasses is also home to the Monastery of the Temple of the Twelve. The monastery is a collection of many smaller buildings surrounding an imposing castle-like structure. The monastery complex is spread over several hills and is legendary in the lore of the people of this world. Some revere it while some say it does not exist at all. The planet has an oxygen/nitrogen-rich atmosphere that is very similar to the atmosphere on our own world of Earth. Like the planet Earth, Chroinia has a slight ten-degree tilt to its rotational axis that results in different seasons on the planets surface as it completes its yearly orbit around the host star. In ages past the people populating this world lived in small villages and cherished the old ways. Magic was

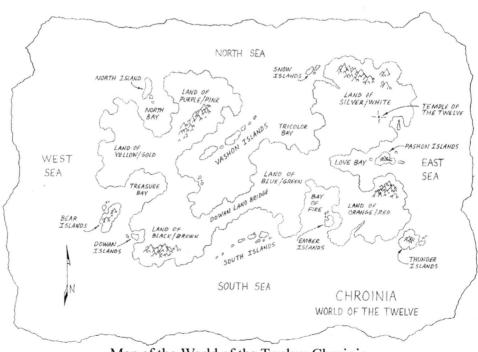

Map of the World of the Twelve: Chroinia
(see page 74 for large map)

a way of life for the people of Chroinia. There was a closeness and oneness to nature that the people cherished above all else. The colors of the Twelve were highly honored and revered in the lives of the people. Becoming a priest or priestess of the Twelve was a highly sought after goal and brought much honor to a family. But times change, and change has come to Chroinia. The people have begun to leave the small villages and congregate in larger villages and cities. Industrialization has begun to take hold. The people now look to machines to free them of the old ways. New ways of thinking and new spiritualities have begun to spring up amongst the people. "How quaint" is the term that many use to describe the old ways and the Temple of the Twelve. There are now many amongst the people who believe that the Temple of the Twelve and the Colors are just stories for children. There are clans and tribes in remote areas that still hold to and practice the old ways. Caroline's sister, Flight, lives with one of these clans. However, the lure of the new and the cities draw the youth away from their elders, so that these remote outposts of the old ways grow smaller each year. The story of Caroline and the Temple of the Twelve takes place in this time of change on Chroinia.

COLOR AND THE TEMPLE
OF THE TWELVE

By assigning specific colors to aspects of the Divine, Temple of the Twelve explores how we as human beings use the cultural, spiritual and psychological aspects of color. The author has incorporated much of the western religious, folk and magical perceptions of color in exploring how Caroline responds to challenges posed by Divinity represented as twelve colors as defined in the story.

The purpose of this journal is to allow you the reader to follow along with Caroline and by extension explore your own psychological, cultural and spiritual relationship to both the perception of color and the Divine.

To help you, the reader, along in this process of exploration, you will have two guides who will assist you. Let's journey to the Monastery of the Twelve and meet them. The Monastery of the Twelve is a large, castle-like structure that commands the top of a wooded hill. The towers and turrets of the monastery are brightly festooned with flags and banners of the twelve colors all dancing in the breeze. You hear the soft tinkling of wind chimes as you near the building and the soft pleasing scent of perfumed incense tickles your senses. As we enter the large wooden door at the monastery entrance, a novitiate of the Twelve greets us and we are ushered into a large library. Large, comfortable, overstuffed chairs are clustered about a huge stone fireplace. There is a warm, welcoming fire in the fireplace which illuminates the library with a soft, flickering glow. Colorful banners of the Twelve decorate the walls not covered by floor to ceiling bookcases. Two figures rise from the chairs to greet us. One figure is a man dressed in a magnificent blue robe with stripes of silver, pink and red. A silver lightning bolt dangles from the end of chain around his neck. A large mane of white hair blends into a long white beard which frames twinkling eyes and a gentle, warm smile. The other figure is a somewhat shorter woman also dressed in the most magnificent robe of many shades of red with splashes of pink, blue and orange. She also wears a silver lightning bolt from a chain around her neck. You notice that she also has a tiny pink heart in the middle of her forehead. Her white hair is done up in a bun on the back of her head and fastened in place with a colorful scarf. Her rosy cheeks frame a warm loving smile.

"Welcome, seekers, to the Monastery of the Temple of the Twelve," the man says in a deep, calming voice.

"Yes. Welcome. We are so glad you are here," says the woman. "Please do sit down and make yourselves comfortable before the fire."

"My dear, can you bring our guests some refreshment?" the woman asks the novitiate waiting at the door.

Soon you are sipping a warm delicious brew

and munching on small sweet cakes. You feel totally at peace and at home.

AND SO THE ADVENTURE OF THE TEMPLE OF THE TWELVE BEGINS

"We understand that you wish to learn about the Temple of the Twelve," says the male figure. "My wife and I will be your guides on your adventure of discovery. Let me introduce myself. I am Gawen, a priest of Blue and Silver, Pink and Red. My lovely wife Caroline, who you have met, is a priestess also of Red and of Pink, Blue and Orange. If you are comfortable, lets us begin your adventure."

Caroline leans forward and says, "Before you read Chapter One of the book, we would like you to create for us a portrait of yourself. Use the space provided on the next page of this workbook to draw your self-portrait. This portrait can be a drawing, a poem, a short narrative, or whatever descriptive form you wish to use."

Gawen strokes his beard and says, "It is important that you be as honest as you can in describing yourself as you see yourself at this point in time. At the end of the workbook you will be asked to describe yourself once again in light of your adventure within the Temple of the Twelve."

CREATE YOUR SELF PORTRAIT

Self Portrait at the Beginning of My Journey

"My goodness, what an interesting and excellent portrait!" exclaims Caroline. Gawen nods his head in approval.

"Now we would like you to read Chapter One of the Temple of The Twelve. When you have finished your reading, come back to this place and we will discuss and explore what you discovered," says Gawen.

Caroline takes a sip from her cup and says, "After you read each chapter you will be given a task to complete right along with the characters in the book. When you complete each task, you will be awarded a color feather, just as the characters in the book earn their color feathers.

An achievement page is provided at the end of this experiential journal for you to color your feathers as you progress through the adventure of the Temple of the Twelve."

READ CHAPTER ONE

Chapter One
The Depth of Black

"Welcome back, dear reader," says Caroline with a smile and a hug. "So let's talk about what you found in Chapter One."

"We will be asking you some questions to better help you interpret what you have read in the light of your own life and circumstances," says Gawen as he motions toward a small table. A copy of the experiential journal lies on the table and is open to the page you are now reading. "Feel free to write your responses, much as you would in a personal journal, in the spaces provided."

Caroline pours some fresh hot tea for everyone, sits back down, takes a sip and says, "In the story, Little Bird meets Black and is challenged to discover who her authentic, real self is."

Gawen continues, "How well do you know your own authentic self? We asked you to create a portrait of your self at the beginning of this adventure. How well do you think that portrait describes your real, authentic self?"

Gawen takes a long sip of warm tea and continues, "After having read Chapter One and meeting Black, is there anything that you would add to your initial portrait? Or perhaps remove?"

_____
_____
_____
_____
_____

"Little Bird of the story has been gifted with artistic talent. What would you say are your own gifts and talents?

_____
_____
_____
_____
_____

Do you feel you have fully explored them? Why or why not?

_____
_____
_____
_____
_____

Temple of the Twelve

"And how do you think Black would encourage you to explore the depths of those gifts and talents? What would she ask you to do with them?" asks Caroline.

_____
_____
_____
_____
_____

(Use additional sheets of paper if you need to. Just insert them into this section of the journal).

"Some people are afraid of Black, thinking it is evil," says Caroline sadly. "Dear reader, do you feel any fear towards Black? If so, why?"

_____
_____
_____
_____
_____

"You have seen how Caroline reacts and interacts with Deity as represented by the color Black. If you were in Little Bird's place, how do you think you would react and interact with the color Black?" asks Caroline.

_____
_____
_____
_____
_____

Gawen leans forward and says, "Select just one of the gifts and talents that you listed earlier, and in the spaces provided write down your plan on how you will improve that gift or talent."

_____
_____
_____
_____

PRAYER TO BLACK

Lady Black, mighty and infinite one from whom all things begin and to whom all things return, teach me not to be afraid of the dark. Please fill me with the understanding that the dark is the balance for the light. The dark does not block the light, but, if used correctly, helps us to see more deeply

Guide me through ever-deepening levels of myself that I might become the spirit I was created to be.

Lady Black, as you are in the center of my eyes, so too you are in the center of my spirit. Tenderly and lovingly I shall always keep you at my center and my source.

In all that I am, in all that I do, may I serve Black.

OPTIONAL: Write Your Own Prayer to Black Here:

_____
_____
_____
_____
_____
_____
_____
_____
_____
_____
_____
_____
_____
_____
_____
_____
_____

A RITUAL FOR BLACK

On the night of the Dark Moon, which is Black's special time, take a black candle and carve something into it that represents a situation in your life that you would like to release. You can write words such as fear, sickness, guilt, etc. You can carve any symbol that means something to you.

As the black candle burns down, visualize Black taking the thing you are releasing into herself. Ask her to transform it into something positive.

Looking into the flame, ask Black what you need to do to help transform the situation. Write her answer here:

_____
_____
_____
_____

"Promise yourself and Black that you will follow through with your plan, and then locate the achievement page at the end of this journal and color one of the feather symbols black," says Caroline.

Gawen strokes his beard and says, "Now that we have seen Little Bird learn how well she knows herself and how to get in touch with her real, authentic self, new challenges await you, dear reader, and our heroine in the next chapter of Temple of The Twelve."

READ CHAPTER TWO

Chapter Two
The Caring of Pink

"Welcome back, dear reader. In Chapter Two, Little Bird meets Pink and is challenged to examine the hurts in her life and how to heal those hurts," says Caroline, while she pours you another cup of the delicious warm tea. Caroline continues, "As you have read in this chapter, Little Bird was given the task to find her three greatest heart wounds and begin to heal them. Before we discuss your greatest heart wounds, let's talk of Pink, as she is much different from Black." Caroline takes another sip of tea and continues, "How do you feel about Pink; what does this color mean to you?"

_____
_____
_____
_____

Gawen says, "Pink is the color of compassion. Do you, dear reader, consider yourself to be a kind and compassionate person? Why or why not?"

_____

"If you were in similar situations as Little Bird, how would your response be different or the same?"

_____
_____
_____
_____
_____

Caroline asks, "Tell me, my friend, do you feel you have treated yourself with gentle compassion throughout your life?"

_____
_____
_____
_____
_____

"Some people think that because Pink is so gentle, she is not a strong color. Do you think of Pink as strong or weak?" asks Caroline.

_____
_____
_____
_____

Gawen looks at you thoughtfully and then says, "What, dear reader, do you think are your three greatest heart wounds?"

_____
_____
_____
_____

Caroline sits back in her chair and asks gently, "Which of the three you have listed would you say is your greatest heart wound?"

_____
_____
_____
_____

"What of your other two greatest heart wounds?" asks Gawen. "How would you describe the healing for these to Pink?"

_____
_____
_____
_____

(Use extra paper if you need to; just place the extra pages at this point in the experiential journal.)

Caroline leans forward and says, "Let us return to your single greatest heart wound and in the spaces provided, and write down your plan to heal that heart wound. I offer you a blessing as you begin this healing. Remember Pink is always with you."

_____
_____
_____
_____
_____
_____
_____
_____

PRAYER TO PINK

Lady Pink, bring me your gentleness and compassion, teach me how to be sensitive and loving towards all living beings, including myself. When I am too harsh on myself or others, fill me with your tender counsel.

Please help me to be unafraid to feel. I want to feel everything from the most exquisite joy to the most profound pain. I want this in order that I might be whole. With your hand in mine, I will not run from love, or from the coldness of hatred, but face both with inner trust.

I believe that I was created to love - to love in everything I do and everything I am. Pink of the Twelve, please help me never forget that above all things, my highest and truest destiny is to be a lover.

May love in me grow with every breath I take.

In all that I as, in all that I do, may I serve Pink.

Temple of the Twelve

OPTIONAL: Write Your Own Prayer to Pink:

A GIFT FOR PINK

Pink represents love, caring and compassion. If you'd like to be closer to Pink, spend a month with her, and every day for a month, do something kind for someone else. It can as simple as a kind word or a smile.

Record your gifts to Pink here:

Day   My gift to Pink

1. _____
2. _____
3. _____
4. _____
5. _____
6. _____
7. _____
8. _____
9. _____
10. _____
11. _____
12. _____
13. _____
14. _____

Experiential Journal

15. _____
_____
_____

16. _____
_____
_____

17. _____
_____
_____

18. _____
_____
_____

19. _____
_____
_____

20. _____
_____
_____

21. _____
_____
_____

22. _____
_____
_____

23. _____
_____
_____

24. _____
_____
_____

25. _____
_____
_____

26. _____
_____
_____

27. _____
_____
_____

28. _____
_____
_____

29. _____
_____
_____

30. _____
_____
_____

31. _____
_____
_____

Caroline continues, "Promise yourself and Pink that you will follow through with your plan, and then locate the achievement page at the end of this journal and color one of the feather symbols pink."

"New magical adventures await you, dear reader, and Little Bird in Chapter Three," says Gawen with a smile. "Let us go out to the main garden and enjoy this beautiful day," he continues. "When you have finished reading Chapter Three, come back and meet us in the garden."

READ CHAPTER THREE

Chapter Three
The Magic of Silver

The main garden of the Temple of the Twelve, located at the base of the hill of novices, is a large, complex arrangement of colorful flowers, bushes and trees affording every texture and color green imaginable. You find Caroline and Gawen waiting for you in the shade of a large old oak tree. Comfortable-looking chairs have been arranged next to a small, gurgling fountain. Colorful flowers burst forth from the ground like so many multi-colored fireworks.

"Come sit and share what you found in Chapter Three," says Caroline, rising to greet you. Gawen pours cups of tea for everyone. A novitiate of the Temple of the Twelve silently brings a large plate of sweet cakes and sets them on the table next to the fountain.

"Thank you, that will be all," says Gawen, and the young novitiate silently departs.

Caroline leans forward and says, "How did you feel inside of yourself when Little Bird first met Silver and learned of magic?"

_____

_____

_____

_____

_____

Gawen leans back in his chair, takes a sip of tea and says, "Silver changes everything he touches. Nothing remains the same after he has interacted with it. We would like you to meditate on your feelings about Silver and then record how you think you have been changed having interacted with Silver through Little Bird."

_____

_____

_____

_____

_____

Caroline then asks, "How do you feel about the concept of magic as described in this chapter?"

_____

_____

_____

Gawen looks thoughtful, then smiles and says, "Gentle reader, what do you think are your magical strengths? And how have you used these gifts to help others, much as Little Bird helped Susannah in the Temple of Brown?"

_____
_____
_____
_____
_____

Caroline adds, "Many people do not believe they have magical gifts. Little Bird struggled with this. Do you struggle with this as well?"

_____
_____

Caroline says, "Silver opened Little Bird to Spirit Travels. What does Spirit Traveling mean to you personally? Is it the same or different than what Little Bird experienced?

_____
_____
_____
_____

What have your own Spirit Travels been like? Remember there are no right or wrong answers, just answers from the heart."

_____
_____
_____
_____
_____

"What aspect of magical power and strength do you feel needs development in your own life?" asks Gawen, looking somewhat serious. "Where do you feel your own magical weaknesses lie?

_____
_____
_____
_____
_____
_____
_____

How can you strengthen them, what can you begin to change?"

_____
_____
_____
_____
_____
_____

PRAYER TO SILVER

Silver, you are the stars in the sky, beckoning me to other worlds. You are the hair of my elders, the wise ones I revere, symbol of their transformation.

You are the coins in my hand with which I can create and manifest my dreams. You are the fish glittering in the lake, the fur of the silver fox in the woods, and the feathers of some birds, for you live in all worlds.

You are the moonlight by which I am blessed. You are the adornment around my neck and fingers, the symbol of commitment and love.

You are the huge rocket ships and medical machines keeping people alive. You are the knife which can be a weapon or cut food. You are the magic and the magician.

By these things shall I learn to understand you, always open to the new dimensions you take me to.

In all that I am, in all that I do, may I serve Silver.

OPTIONAL: Write Your Own Prayer to Silver:

_____

Temple of the Twelve

15. Totem Animal Guides
16. Aura reading
17. Hypnosis
18. Crystals, Minerals and Metals
19. Astral Travel
20. Empathy

Spend a month — it would be wonderful if it was a New Moon to the next New Moon — and study your chosen magical art. Record your findings and observations in a notebook or your computer. Summarize here.

_____

A LESSON WITH SILVER

Please choose one of the following magical arts that you wish to know more about.

1. Astrology
2. Tarot
3. Runes
4. Scrying
5. Herbology
6. Numerology
7. Pendulum
8. Dream Analysis
9. Reiki
10. Mediumship (Connecting to the Other Side)
11. Guided Meditation/Journeying
12. Telepathy
13. Healing
14. Past Life Recall

"After you promise Silver you will work on your magical needs, locate the achievement page at the end of this journal and color one of the feather symbols silver," says Caroline with a big smile.

"You have done well, dear reader," says Gawen, "but more loving adventures await you in the next chapter. Caroline and I will meet you back here in the garden after you read Chapter Four."

READ CHAPTER FOUR

Chapter Four
The Wisdom of Blue

"Welcome back, dear reader. Please come sit with us and share what you found in Chapter Four," says Gawen, extending a hand to help you to your chair. A small table next to your chair holds a small plate with baked sweets and a large mug.

"You simply must try this new herbal tea blend," says Caroline as she pours a steaming beverage into the large mug. Caroline pours some of the hot tea for herself and Gawen and then sits down in her own chair. You take a sip of the hot tea and find it mellow and pleasantly sweet. It is good to be with Caroline and Gawen, enjoying the tea in the garden and the pleasant company of each other.

After taking a sip of the tea, Caroline continues, "In Chapter ofur of the story, Little Bird meets Blue and is challenged to let herself be loved by the Divine. When Little Bird first meets Blue she is told a vital, profound truth - Deity comes alive through us as perceiving human beings."

Gawen leans forward in his chair, takes a sweet from the plate, and asks, "How do you think Deity comes alive through you, dear reader?"

_____
_____
_____
_____
_____

Caroline leans back in her chair and says, "In Chapter Four of the story, Little Bird meets Gawen's grandfather who has passed beyond and consented to visit them for one time, to share a message of love and hope. If you could speak to a loved one who has passed beyond, what would you like to say to them and what do you imagine that they would say to you?"

_____
_____
_____
_____
_____

Gawen strokes his white beard and says in a low, thoughtful voice, "In the story, Little Bird sees a picture of herself painted by the Divine represented by Blue. In the story, Little Bird runs away thinking that she is unworthy and could never measure up to the image of her as seen by the Divine." Gawen looks very thoughtful and then says, "If you were to meet Blue and a picture was painted of you showing you in all your beauty and goodness, would you too run away thinking yourself unworthy? Or would your reaction be different?"

_____
_____
_____
_____
_____

Caroline, who had been looking at Gawen intently, now turns her gaze toward you. With a thoughtful tone she says in a soft, reverent voice, "Have you, dear reader, ever run away from a loving gift that the Divine wanted to give you?

_____
_____
_____
_____
_____

And did you, like Little Bird in the story, finally find the courage and love to accept that gift in the end? Or perhaps there is a gift that the Divine has offered that you have yet to accept?"

_____
_____
_____
_____
_____

Gawen takes a sip of his tea and looks at Caroline. Caroline smiles and nods her head, then Gawen turns toward you and says, "Dear reader, remember that the Divine sees through us, but it is our perception that brings Divinity to life."

Gawen continues, "We would like you to do as Little Bird was told to by Blue. Imagine that you are in a long hallway. Walk down it. There is a door at the end. Open it. We would like you to imagine that you see a large picture on the wall in front of you. At first it is blank. An image begins to form in the blank picture. The image will be what you need to see. Do you see the image? Briefly describe what you see."

_____
_____
_____
_____
_____

"Now imagine a wave of pure Blue. It can be water or wind, but it is clear and pure. Imagine it washing through you, carrying off the negativity; doubt, fear, lack of focus: whatever troubles you. Let the wave pass through you until you feel clean, sparkling clean. Crystal clean."

Caroline, who had been listening intently, now says, "Take the image that you saw in the picture and make it your own, and color it with your own thoughts, prayers and wishes. How would you help Blue see this vision?"

_____
_____
_____
_____
_____

"Promise Blue that you will continue to work on helping him see through your eyes, and then locate the achievement page at the end of this journal and color one of the feather symbols blue."

PRAYER TO BLUE

Lord Blue, grant me clear vision. May I see truly with the eyes of my body, and the eyes of my spirit. Help me to see through all illusion, that I might be filled with only truth.

Enter into my spirit and teach me the ways of peace. Teach me to live in trust, relaxing in the love of the universe. May I radiate the tranquility of a quiet lake in all I do. At my very center, no matter what is going on around me, may I be at peace.

Teach me also the ways of a storm. Please help me to rise up in force when my passion, anger, or determination is called for. The sky and the sea change from stillness to storm as they need it. Stir me, Lord Blue, to care.

You are the Lord of visions. Grant me a vision of the future as you would wish it to be. Help me to dream. Help me to imagine. Take me into the future, into new horizons, destinies and adventures. Remind me that there is always a tomorrow. Create in me a questing, seeking, curious heart.

May my words be clear and true. May I communicate who I am to others without misunderstanding and with integrity. May I never forget to say I love you.

In all that I am, in all that I do, may I serve Blue.

OPTIONAL: Write Your Own Prayer to Blue:

_____
_____
_____
_____
_____
_____
_____
_____
_____
_____
_____
_____

CREATING WITH BLUE

Blue is about self-expression. What art form have you always longed to pursue? Painting, writing, acting, dancing, pottery, playing a musical instrument? Or what art form have you begun to pursue, but have not paid enough attention to?

_____
_____
_____
_____
_____
_____
_____
_____
_____

Resolve to bring this art form more fully into your life. Make no excuses about time or money. Take baby steps if necessary, but take them. Become the more creative person you were meant to be. Record your adventure with Blue here.

_____
_____
_____
_____
_____
_____
_____
_____
_____
_____

A LETTER FOR BLUE

Blue is Lord of Communication. Write someone a letter, telling them clearly how you feel about them. Record your letter, the adventure of writing it, and giving it, here. Keep a copy of the letter here by slipping it into the workbook.

"You have done well, dear reader," says

Gawen with a big smile. "But new adventures of passion and pleasure await you in the next two chapters."

"After you have read Chapters Five and Six, meet us on top of the Hill of Novices. There you will find us in a circle of stones," says Caroline, as both she and Gawen rise to leave the garden.

"See you soon in the circle of stones," they both say in unison as they wave good-bye to you.

READ CHAPTERS
FIVE AND SIX

Chapter Five & Six
The Passion of Red and The Life of Green

It is a pleasantly warm early afternoon and the sun is high in a clear blue, cloudless sky. After the long hike up the Hill of Novices, you see Gawen and Caroline sitting on a large blanket spread out in the center of a stone circle.

Gawen rises to greet you and says, "Welcome back, dear reader. Come sit with us and tell us of your adventure with Red and Green." You find a comfortable spot on the blanket and sit down between your two guides, Gawen and Caroline. Arrayed before you, on the blanket are small sandwiches and fruit set out on pretty red and green plates. Caroline hands you a cup filled with a cool, sweet beverage. You take a sip and find it very refreshing after your long trek up the hill.

Caroline takes a sip from her cup and asks you, "We are interested in your interactions with Red. If you were to meet Lady Red as you are today, how do you think she would appear to you?"

_____
_____
_____
_____

Gawen, resting on his side of the blanket says, "I am interested in your perception of Green. If you were to meet Lady Green as you are today, how do you think she would appear to you?

_____
_____
_____
_____
_____

Gawen looks at Caroline as if an unspoken communication had just passed between them, and then looks at you and says, "What do you think Lady Red represents for you in your life?"

_____
_____
_____
_____
_____

Caroline then says, "Likewise, what do you think Lady Green represents for you in your life?"

Temple of the Twelve

_____
_____
_____
_____
_____

Gawen strokes his beard and says, "Dear reader, if Lady Red were to ask you why you are here in this life and how you can best serve the Divine, how would you answer Lady Red?"

_____
_____
_____
_____
_____

Caroline sits up on the blanket and, looking directly at you the reader, says, "So now, dear reader, next comes a most difficult question, one that may require some serious thought. The question is the same posed by Lady Green to Little Bird in the story; that is, what are your three greatest pleasures, and most importantly, why are these three your greatest pleasures?"

My greatest pleasure is:

_____
_____
_____
_____

Why is this your greatest pleasure?

_____
_____
_____
_____
_____

My second greatest pleasure is:

_____

Why is this your second greatest pleasure?

_____
_____
_____
_____
_____

My third greatest pleasure is:

_____
_____
_____
_____

Why is this your third greatest pleasure?

_____
_____
_____

Caroline takes a long drink from her cup and continues, "If you could retreat to a little cabin the woods, as did Little Bird in Chapter Six of the story, what would you take with you?"

_____
_____
_____
_____
_____

"Just as important, what would you leave behind?"

Gawen moves to sit closer to Caroline and says, "Dear reader, would your purpose in staying in a little cabin in the woods be the same as it was for Little Bird in the story, or would you have a different purpose?"

Gawen raises himself to a sitting position and says, "There is a section of Chapter Six where Pink is speaking to Little Bird about her three heart wounds." He opens the book to a place marked with a red tassel and begins to read.

"The power to heal yourself was always in your own heart and hands and mind and vision. It does not lie outside of you. Go home to yourself. Your home is within your own body. Create your dream. Create it of that magical mysterious star stuff inside that makes you, you. …. Each of us has a voice of truth and life and love and joy that was stolen from us, is too far away from us, that we deem impossible to ever reach again. For the earth, the voice of the sky, which it can never touch, but each of us has a way – a way to bring that voice back to stay ……For some, it could be baking a cake. For some, it could be building a house or dancing. For some, it could be healing the sick. There is always a way to hear once more the voice of the Gods."

Gawen lookes up from the book and says, "Now, dear reader, meditate on this passage and tell us in what way you choose to once again hear the voice of the Gods, to heal yourself, to better create your dream. Feel free to tell us in whatever way you choose, be it a poem, a song, a drawing or whatever way you choose. There is no right or wrong here, just what comes from your own heart."

Caroline makes a blessing sign over you and says, "Speak to the Divine in your own way and resolve to create your own dream, to seek your own destiny by seeking your own voice of truth and life and love and joy."

A DAY WITH GREEN

Plan a day for yourself, from waking up until going to sleep. This day is all for you. Allow yourself to pamper yourself and indulge in your greatest pleasures. Do not allow time constraints or commitments to stop you from taking this single day to devote to pleasures.

What was it like to plan the Day of Pleasures?

What was the Day of Pleasures like for you?

PRAYER TO GREEN

My body is a green growing field; I tend it with love and wisdom that it may flourish.

My life is a garden. I clean it of weeds. I grow the things I need in it. It is a place of beauty. My life is a garden. In it I find sanctuary. I work hard, but it is a place of rest as well.

I am an abundant, vital, alive force. I have the power of creation within me. In cold, barren seasons, I wait without fear for the growing time. The growing time will always come again.

Lady Green, you teach me that all of life is endless possibilities. You create in me a hunger to grow and to keep growing. You awaken the sleeping places and the sleeping dreams within me. You touch the dead and it returns to the world of the living. Teach me to use my energy with an open heart and hand, freely giving of myself. Teach me also wisdom that I might not try to reach too high too fast. Please enter my life and clear it of spiritual dust. Please refresh and renew my creative spirit. All of life is a creative force, even if that force calls for destruction to clear the path.

Lady Green, help me to see the life force in others, and to do all I can to strengthen it. Please heal those parts of me that are ill, both in body and in heart. I am a creature of life. I am a creature of positive creative energy. I am one with the creative force of the Universe.

I hold pleasure and joy as sacred. They are not luxuries and they are not frivolous. They are as essential as air. I live in joy and I seek always to deepen my joy.

I am within the Divine and the Divine is within me. I am beautiful, strong and full of life. Praise to the life force within all of us. My life is an act of praise.

In all I do, in all I am, may I serve Green.

OPTIONAL: Write Your Own Prayer to Green:

_____
_____
_____
_____
_____
_____
_____
_____
_____
_____
_____
_____
_____
_____
_____
_____
_____
_____
_____

Both Gawen and Caroline stand up. Gawen helps you to stand up as well, and says, "Both you and Little Bird in the story have work yet to do with both Red and Green, but you are well on your way. Read Chapter Seven and then meet both Caroline and I back here on the Hill of Novices in the stone circle and we will talk of your further adventures with both Red and Green."

READ CHAPTER SEVEN

Chapter Seven
The Passion of Red and The Life of Green...continued

Once again you make the long trek up the Hill of Novices to the stone circle and this time find Gawen and Caroline sitting in chairs next to a small table. There is an empty chair next to the table toward which Caroline motions for you to sit down. As before, there are red and green plates with a collection of small sweets, and a pitcher containing an iced beverage. Caroline pours you a cup of the beverage that you find very refreshing after your long trek up the hill.

Caroline pours some of the beverage for both herself and Gawen, and then looks at you and says, "Which of the colors is represented in the man Jonathan, whom Little Bird sheltered from the storm in her little cabin?"

_____
_____
_____
_____

Gawen strokes his beard and says, "You will meet Jonathan again later in the story; for now, however, we are curious as to why you feel that Jonathan represents the color you selected?"

_____
_____
_____
_____
_____

Caroline continues, "Would you have reacted to Jonathan the same way Little Bird did, or would you have reacted differently?"

_____
_____
_____
_____
_____

Caroline sits back in her chair and looks at Gawen. He nods back at her as if a non-verbal communication has just taken place. Caroline then says, in a somewhat serious tone of voice, "Dear reader, we would like you to revisit your three greatest pleasures, and this time tell us what they are and why they are your greatest pleasures, in any way you choose. This can be poetry, visual art, music, or what have you. There are no right or wrong answers, as what you record in this journal is from your heart and is to help you reach your own destiny."

_____
_____
_____
_____
_____

Gawen smiles; he comments to Caroline on how moving your response was to the three greatest pleasures. He makes you feel proud.

PRAYER TO RED

I am a warrior(ess) of truth. I stand ready to serve. I am a warrior(ess) who helps those in need.

The Divine is free to use me as one of its defenders. I offer my service in the name of Red. I understand fully the commitment I am making, and I make it with a clear heart.

I love these bright souls (Here name a few of those you love):

_____
_____
_____
_____
_____

And I vow to do all I can to fill their lives with joy and passion. I dedicate myself to them in the name of Red.

I pledge myself to my highest calling (Name it here, if you wish):

_____
_____

I pledge myself to my highest calling in the name of Red.

Blood of my ancestors created me; blood of my legacy shall carry the torch after me. In blood I am born, die and am reborn.

In all I do, in all I am, may I serve Red.

OPTIONAL: Write Your Own Prayer to Red:

_____
_____
_____
_____
_____
_____
_____
_____
_____
_____
_____
_____
_____
_____
_____
_____
_____
_____

A GIFT TO RED

Red is the color of blood for a reason. It represents the life force.

Give of your life force to one who needs it. If possible, (if not for all people) donate blood this week or donate to the Red Cross or a local hospital, or become an organ donor. Dedicate the gift to Red who brings life.

Record your adventure here:

Experiential Journal

A TREE OR FLOWER FOR GREEN

Find a tree or bush, or even some flowers, in your area that call to you. Those with green thumbs might purchase a tree or bush. Every week spend a half hour with it, for as many weeks as you wish. Draw a picture of it, photograph it, hang ribbons in the branches, leave offerings for the fairies there, whatever calls you. Study the type of tree or plant that called you on the Internet. What is most important is that you develop a bond with it. Talk to it (even silently) about your hopes and dreams. Learn from it, be still and quiet, and listen. It will speak to you, even if you don't realize it right away. Cry with it, laugh with it, just be with it.

You might make a wand from a branch, or press some of the leaves in a book to save them. You might clean the area if it is in a littered park. You might take a friend with you to visit your tree or flower. You might play music to it on an instrument or CD player.

This project is completed when you have a strong bond with this tree or flower, but you may return to it anytime you wish. Record your experiences with your tree or flower here.

_____
_____
_____
_____
_____
_____
_____
_____
_____

A CONTRACT WITH RED

Everyone's life is a contract with the Divine. There is a sacred agreement between you and the universe. It explains why you were born, and what you must do to fulfill your highest potential.

Create your contract. Make it beautiful using calligraphy, computer graphics, photos of yourself, a nice frame, pressed flowers, whatever you feel called to do. Just be sure to make it nice - treat it as the sacred thing it is.

Begin your contract with the words,

"I, _____ , enter into this contract with the infinite Universe; I enter into this sacred contract with ALL that is."

Then write what you feel the Universe is truly asking you to do with your life. Record your adventure here:

Gawen looks at you with a big smile and says, "You have come such a long way on your journey with the colors. Promise Red that the red fire of courage, inspiration, strength, and motivation will always burn brightly within you. Then locate the page provided at the end of this journal and color one of the feather symbols red. Congratulations, dear reader!"

Caroline also looks at you with a big smile and says, "I agree with Gawen. You, dear reader, have indeed come far in your journey with the colors. Promise Green that you will always cherish and nurture your greatest pleasures, for you cannot achieve your highest destiny if you are not open to your highest pleasures. Then locate the page provided at the end of this journal and color one of the feather symbols green. Congratulations, dear reader."

Gawen stands up out of his chair, takes your hand in his, and says, "New adventures in companionship and friendship with the Divine await you in the next chapter. After you read Chapter Eight, meet us outside the Chapel of Orange that Little Bird was told to create."

READ CHAPTER EIGHT

Chapter Eight
The Glory of Orange

The Chapel of Orange is a stone structure made of red, orange and brown stones and crystals located in a back quarter of the expansive temple gardens. The Chapel is festooned with vines bearing red and orange flowers. Just outside the chapel, off to one side, in a small grove of trees, you find Gawen and Caroline sitting in chairs at a large stone table made of orange and red stones. Gawen rises and greets you, then directs you to sit in an empty chair opposite them at the table.

"Greetings, dear reader," says Caroline, while pouring you a tall ice-filled glass with amber-colored liquid that looks like iced tea. "Gawen and I are very interested to hear about your adventures with Lord Orange."

Gawen turns in his chair to face you and says, "Dear reader, I am curious about how you interpret the statement of Orange to Little Bird, 'Take your respect and throw in the nearest garbage heap. I don't want respect; I want love, respect is already within love.' "

_____

_____

_____

Caroline takes a drink from her glass and says, "Dear reader, if you were in the place of Little Bird in the story, how would you approach the decoration of the Chapel of Orange?"

_____

_____

_____

_____

_____

Caroline continues, "On page 162 in the story, Lord Orange introduces himself to Little Bird as the Lord of Opposites, the Lord of two sides of the same thing. In this section Lord Orange tells Little Bird, 'Love is always safe, but only if you are prepared to trust with all your heart'. What does this statement mean to you? Remember there are no right or wrong answers - only those from your heart."

_____

_____

Gawen strokes his beard, sits back and says, "As Little Bird saw in the necklace analogy presented to her by lady Red, we are all a part of the Divine and the Divine is all a part of us; one cannot exist without the other. Tell us how, in your life, you will know the Divine as friend, as an integral part of your life, and as an equal partner in this adventure called life."

_____
_____
_____
_____
_____

Caroline smiles at you encouragingly and says, "In your past relationships to Deity, have you considered it a friend, or has it been something distant or fearful to you? Do you focus on the unknowable aspect of Deity, or the aspect you can know? Why do you think this is? Can you think of a time when Deity was very much a best friend to you?"

_____
_____
_____
_____
_____

Caroline looks at you with a serious expression on her face and says, "Dear reader, resolve to take your place not only with Orange, but with Deity as you conceive of it. Imagine and understand yourself to be a part that is irreplaceable, rejoice in being within the Divine as Deity rejoices at being within you. In the place provided below write down how you will do this, and then reward yourself locating the achievement page at the end of this journal and coloring one of the feather symbols orange. Congratulations, dear reader."

_____
_____
_____
_____
_____

A CHAPEL FOR ORANGE

Make your own chapel for Orange, the way Caroline did. It does not have to be a building. Use a cardboard box, or a small table or shelf or a corner of your yard. It can be an orange tree in warmer climates, a fireplace in cooler ones.

Fill it with things that are orange (also red and yellow) and things that make you feel warm, loved, cherished and nurtured. Record your observations here.

_____
_____
_____
_____
_____
_____
_____
_____

PRAYER TO ORANGE

Lord Orange, fill my life with warmth and light. May the rooms of my home ring with joy and laughter no matter what my life's circumstances. I wish to live in bliss, not ignoring the difficulties of life, but not allowing them to rule me, either.

Grant to me a giving and generous heart, so that when I see a person in need, I do what I can to help. Please help me to understand that a successful life is not co-dependent on others, but is always interconnected. We need each other.

Grant me also an understanding of the difference between humility and self-abasement. I love to feel good about myself, despite my faults - and I promise to work on those.

Please remind me that I am never alone. Deity is Father, Mother, Sister and Brother to me. Deity loves me. If I forget how much Deity loves me, please gently bring me back to your warm protection. May I never stray from it.

In all that I am do, in all that I do, may I serve Orange.

OPTIONAL: Write Your Own Prayer to Orange:

_____
_____
_____
_____
_____
_____
_____
_____
_____
_____
_____
_____
_____

AN AFFIRMATION FOR ORANGE

Every day for a month, start the day by looking in the mirror and saying, "Deity (God, Goddess, Creator, etc - choose the word that resonates with you) loves me."

Do this whether or not you believe it - but take note of your reactions, and try to understand why you don't believe it, or don't believe it enough. Try to mean it more and more over the next month. Record your observations here.

_____
_____
_____
_____
_____
_____
_____
_____
_____
_____

Caroline stands up and extends her hand to you and helps you to stand. She says to you, "New adventures in curiosity and learning await you and Little Bird in the next chapter.

After you have read Chapter Nine, meet us in the Scholar's Library and we will discuss your adventures." Caroline then takes Gawen's hand and says, "See you after the next chapter," as they both wave to you and you begin your new quest.

READ CHAPTER NINE

Chapter Nine
The Sacredness of Purple

The Scholar's Library in the Monastery of the Twelve is located on the top floor of this castle-like structure. It is a large room lined with oak bookcases from floor to ceiling and stacked with a dizzying array of books. A series of tables is positioned at the rear of the library. On these tables are a fascinating array of astronomical models and various scientific apparatus. The ceiling is a large dome that can open from the side to reveal the night sky. The library has an aura of hushed learning and scholarship about it.

You gaze around yourself in awe. This place is the dream of every lover of books, every scientist, every scholar of the magical arts, and you take a moment to reflect on how blessed you are to be here.

You find Caroline and Gawen waiting for you. They are sitting at a small, purple-colored table in a back corner of the library. A purple cloth studded with silver stars covers the table and a small plate of sweet cakes sits at its center. A purple pitcher and glasses are arranged at the edges of the table. Gawen arises to greet you and directs you to sit with them.

Caroline pours a beverage from the purple pitcher into one of the glasses and hands it to you. "You will find this refreshing," she said with a smile.

The beverage has a slightly sweet taste and you find your thirst is quenched. You feel strangely relaxed and refreshed. You sit back in the comfortable chair and drink in the hushed energy of the library.

Caroline smiles at you and asks, "How did you find your visit with Purple? If you were in Little Bird's place, would you react the same way as did Little Bird, or would you react differently?"

_____
_____
_____
_____
_____

Gawen then leans back in his chair and says, "Dear reader, Caroline and I are interested in what you feel are your three greatest spiritual wounds. These are similar to the emotional wounds Pink worked on with you, but focused more specifically in the realm of your spiritual life."

Gawen continues, "How would you use what you now know of Purple to help heal those spiritual wounds?"

Caroline leans back in her chair and says, "In this chapter, Purple asks Little Bird to create a ritual that will bring people closer to him. If you were in Little Bird's place, what kind of ritual would you create? Try and describe as much detail as you can, because in so doing it will become more real for you."

Gawen puts a hand on your shoulder and asks, "What have your spiritual studies in this life been like? Were they pleasant and fulfilling or did they leave you still seeking? Who do you feel are your greatest spiritual teachers?"

Looking at you with curiosity in her eyes, Caroline asks, "Have you found it easier to study spiritual matters in a group, or on your own? Do you feel you have support for your spirituality in your life?"

Caroline continues, "If you could 'unlearn' anything that you learned about spirituality in the past, what would it be? If you could learn something in the spiritual realms that you always wanted to learn, but never did, what would it be?"

Gawen leans forward in his chair and says, "Purple takes Little Bird on a journey to his Kingdom of Purple. We would like you to take what you now know of Purple and take your own inner meditative journey to the Kingdom of Purple. In the spaces provided below, describe as best you can what you see on this meditative journey."

A SPIRITUAL QUEST WITH PURPLE

Study another spiritual path, one that you don't know all that much about. You can simply read about it, or you can go farther and visit a place of worship in the faith you are studying. You can interview someone of that faith. What did you learn?

A PRAYER TO PURPLE

I am a spark from the Divine Fire. As such, I am forever seeking my way back to union with that Fire. There is a primal, raw part of me that understands that if I do not stay connected to my Source, I will eventually flicker out and die. I may burn brilliantly for a while, but eventually I will die out. I need the constant renewal from my Source.

Yes, sometimes it scares me because I am afraid I will get lost in the whole. So sometimes I get so far away from the Source that I fear I'll never find my way back. I have had moments where I was so lost I had no idea how to find my way back.

There is a surrender that comes with understanding that I am only a spark of that fire. I am not able to fully comprehend the brilliance, the magnificence of the One. All I can do is shine in my little corner of the darkness.

I drape myself in the purple of Divinity. I must never forget who I am. I am a child of the Divine. I am doing the work of my father and mother, the One. I am their messenger, their instrument, and their deeply beloved.

I am a spark from the Divine Fire.

In all that I am, in all that I do, may I serve Purple.

OPTIONAL: Write Your Own Prayer to Purple:

Gawen smiles, and says, "Remember, dear reader, you may return to that magical place whenever you wish. Both Caroline and I would like you to promise Purple that you will use the understandings gained in this chapter to continue healing your three greatest spiritual wounds. Locate the achievement page at the back of this journal and color one of the feather symbols purple. Congratulations, dear reader."

Caroline says with a wry smile, "And now, dear reader, new adventures with Brown await you in the next chapter. After you read the next chapter, Gawen and I will meet you in the tree-lined circle in the sacred glade on the back Temple grounds to discuss your adventure with Brown. May your journey be good one." They both wave good-bye to you as you walk away in search of Brown.

READ CHAPTER TEN

Chapter Ten
The Security of Brown

Located in a secluded glade on the back grounds of the monastery, you find a large circle of ancient oak trees. Their thick, gnarled, timeworn trunks are evenly spaced, giving the appearance of ancient warriors standing guard. The evenly spaced tree trunks create a perfect circle about 100 feet in diameter and interlocking tree canopies. As you walk toward the center of the circle where Caroline and Gawen are waiting for you; a warm comforting wave of sacred truth washes over you. This wave of sacred truth seems to fill and permeate the sacred space. At the center of the circle you find seats and a table hewn out of the living rock. Stoneware plates piled high with fruits of the Earth, a large earthenware pot filled with a rich brown steaming liquid, and stoneware mugs sit on the table.

Gawen rises to greet you. "Welcome, dear reader. I trust you had a great adventure with Brown? Caroline and I are eager to hear all about it and we have some questions for you to ponder as well. Come sit, enjoy the fruits of the Earth and share with us."

Caroline pours some of the rich brown steaming liquid into a mug and hands it to you and says, "This will warm you and refresh your spirit."

You sip the steaming brown liquid and find that it tastes much like rich hot chocolate. You find yourself relaxed and strangely comfortable on the stone seat.

Gawen leans forward in his seat and says, "If you were in Little Bird's place meeting Brown for the first time, would you find yourself staring at Brown? And how would you react to the straightforward, rather blunt nature of Brown?"

_____
_____
_____
_____
_____

Caroline then asks, "Brown asked Little Bird to find out whether love is something you always have to ask for, or is it given to you. What assumptions come with love, if any? After having read how Little Bird handles this investigation, we would like your views on this question. In other words, do you agree with what Little Bird found, or are your views different? Remember there are no right or wrong answers here."

Gawen takes a sip from his mug and asks, "Brown also asked Little Bird to investigate questions about how honest one must be with another. And what is helpful, courteous criticism and unkind criticism? We would like your views on these two questions. Have there been times in your own life where these questions have become important?"

Caroline smiles and says, "In her conversations with her mother, Little Bird found the first rule of love which was to pay attention to those you love. How have you found this first rule applicable to your own life, dear reader?"

Gawen then said, "Little Bird found that rule number two for love was to give and that two other rules were keep it simple and remember what matters. Although appearing simple, these concepts are sometimes forgotten. In that light, how do these rules apply in your own life, dear reader?"

Caroline leans forward in her seat and says, "Little Bird also discovered another important concept concerning love and relationships with others. She called this concept seek your true happiness. With this thought in mind, how, dear reader, would you describe your own true happiness?"

Gawen nods to Caroline and says, "After her visit with Rhyanna and Zachary in the little cabin, Little Bird discovers that love is so giving that it is simply always there for us. Our mistakes, it transforms into truth and wisdom. Our cruelty it heals. The question of love is not what do I need to ask for. It is, what have I been given? Am I seeing it? Now, dear reader, examine your own life. Is there love in your life that you have not yet seen?"

Caroline looks at you with curiosity and says,

Temple of the Twelve

"In your life, dear reader, have you been able to be close to the earth? Do you feel that you live separated from nature or very connected to it? What might you do to be closer to the earth?"

_____
_____
_____
_____
_____

A PRAYER TO BROWN

Lord Brown, Lord of the forests and the wild animals, Lord of the earth and the gardens, he who runs with the deer and wolf, be here with me now.

Center me, grant to me the feeling that my feet are connected to the earth beneath them. Grant me the certain knowing that comes when my life spark is glowing right in the center of my belly.

Keep me aware of all things around me, as the rabbit is aware of the scent of grass and the fox. Instill in me knowledge of the dignity and sacredness of all living things. Grant me such openness that the dandelion speaks to me and I can hear.

Lord of wood. Lord of stone, you are the master builder. May I look to you for guidance when I am structuring my home and my life, and create a firm foundation. May I take pride in my work and do it well.

Lord Brown, bringer of truth and reality, help me to live in the world that is. Help me to see it rightly and without illusion. With your hand in mine I shall live an ethical life, a life of integrity and honor. I shall not demean my bright spirit with immorality and poor action.

Lord Brown, you are the warmth of fresh pumpkin bread and the sharpness of jagged cliffs. I follow you home, to my true home, and my true center.

In all that I am, in all that I do, may I serve Brown.

OPTIONAL: Write Your Own Prayer to Brown:

_____
_____
_____
_____
_____
_____
_____
_____
_____
_____
_____
_____
_____
_____
_____
_____

A CLEAN HOME AND STRONG BODY FOR BROWN

Brown is the color of earth, and one of the things that earth represents is home. As the birds make nests and the bears find caves, so we seek a nook and cranny of Mother Earth to call our safe and secure place.

Does your home reflect who you really are?

_____
_____
_____
_____
_____

Take a weekend and make one room of your home more in tune with your vision and ideal for it. How does this fixed-up room clear your mind and spirit?

Experiential Journal

_____
_____
_____
_____
_____

Brown also represents the physical, your body. How can you better your health? Take one step towards taking better care of your body. Write about your experience here.

READ CHAPTER ELEVEN

_____
_____
_____
_____
_____
_____
_____
_____
_____

Caroline stands up, extends her hand to you, and invites you to stand as well. "Promise Brown that you will continue to seek the love that is all around you and live in beauty and truth. Locate the achievement page at the back of this journal and color one of the feather symbols brown. Congratulations, dear reader."

Gawen arises from his seat and says, "New adventures await you in the next chapter where you will meet the color White. After you have read Chapter Eleven we will meet you in the Chapel of White in the back Temple gardens. Until then, good journey to you." He waves to you as you walk out of the circle of trees on your way to meet White.

Chapter Eleven
The Rebirth of White

You find the Chapel of White as a small building made of white marble located in a small wooded glade on the back grounds of the Temple monastery. As you walk into the chapel you find the inside a glittering white, the walls seeming to glow softly, illuminating the inside with a warm soft light. Large bouquets of white roses decorate the altar at the back of the Chapel. There is a soft sense of great reverence and happy innocence about this sacred space. There are comfortable seats positioned as a circle in the center of the Chapel. You find Caroline and Gawen sitting at a small white table in the back of the Chapel, waiting for you. There is a white plate at the center of the table loaded with a variety of sweet cakes coated with sparkling sugar. Caroline is pouring you a sparkling, bubbly beverage into a tall, crystal drinking glass.

"Welcome, dear reader," says Caroline, and she motions for you to sit at the table. "Gawen and I are interested to hear of your adventure with White."

You thank Caroline and sit in one of the chairs by the table. You take a sip of the sparkling bubbly beverage and find it refreshes body and mind. You are refreshed and relaxed in the beautiful Chapel of White.

Caroline leans forward in her chair and asks, "Now that you have shared Little Bird's adventure, what is your personal view of the concept of innocence? Do you feel that you, in your life, have been created and recreated innocent, over and over again?"

_____
_____
_____
_____
_____

Gawen then says, "Little Bird was given a great challenge by White to work with Tara to help her recreate her innocence and learn to love. Would you have handled this challenge the same way as Little Bird or would your approach have been different?"

_____
_____
_____

Caroline takes a sip from her drink and says, "Dear reader, as Little Bird rode the Ferris wheel to the top and released the balloon to let go of her moment, what moment in your life would you release if you were atop the Ferris wheel with your balloon?"

_____

_____

_____

_____

Gawen gives you a serious look and says, "If you were to ride in White's silver sleigh and fly away with White to her kingdom, describe what you think you would see on that journey."

_____

_____

_____

_____

Caroline looks very thoughtful and asks, "Dear reader, what do you think of Tara's dilemma with the dark ones? Do you, in your life, have a similar dilemma? Or do you know of someone who suffers as Tara does? How would you help yourself or this other person in your life?"

_____

_____

_____

_____

Gawen strokes his beard and then looks directly at you and says, "From your reading about Little Bird's adventure with White, what wisdom concerning innocence and love do you now have that you did not have before?"

_____

_____

_____

_____

A PRAYER TO WHITE

White Lady of snow and ice, bless me, please, with your purity. Little white edelweiss flower, growing high in the mountains, I quest for your purity within me.

White Lady, look at my eyes. At the center is black, surrounding black is color – and surrounding the color is you. Your radiance and light enfold me.

Please help me to understand that I was born pure and innocent, and this is my true nature. It seems hard to pursue purity and innocence, but it is harder not to do so, for they are my nature. They are the true nature of all living things.

White Lady, Black is not bad while you are good. Help me to understand that I will not find you by turning my back on the velvet night.

Immaculate One, unstained and pristine, I am afraid of your cold side. White Queen, your seasons of ice and snow will not destroy me, but will instead strengthen me.

White Swan, gracefully flowing down a river, white clouds flowing through the sky, you are the eternal bride. You are ever the virgin like new fallen snow. At the same time you are the white beard of the old Sage. Spiritual virginity is not being untouched. It is eternal renewal, eternal wholeness.

White angel, white ballerina, white fairy, white princess, white rose, I adore your shining glory.

In all that I am and in all I do, may I serve White.

Temple of the Twelve

OPTIONAL: Write Your Own Prayer to White:

_____
_____
_____
_____
_____
_____
_____
_____
_____
_____
_____
_____
_____
_____
_____
_____

Caroline and Gawen look at each other and then turn toward you. Caroline says, "You have done well, dear reader. Promise White that you will continue your work toward the rebirth of innocence and love in your own life, and then locate the achievement page at the back of this journal and color one of the feather symbols white. Congratulations, dear reader."

Gawen gets up out of his seat and says, "New bold adventures with Gold await you in the next chapter. We will meet you in the Chapel of Gold in the back garden of the Temple monastery after you have read the next chapter."

"We look forward to sharing your adventures with Gold," says Caroline with a broad smile as she gets up from her seat and takes Gawen's arm. She turns and says, "Farewell for now," and walks with Gawen out of the Chapel of White.

AN OUTFIT FOR WHITE

For one day, wear only white: White dress, shoes, pants, underclothing, robes, whatever you have. Wear no other color at all.

See how it makes you feel, and take note of your reactions. Are you comfortable in all white? Why or why not?

_____
_____
_____
_____

How does it affect your mood and actions? How does it affect how others perceive you? Or act towards you?

_____
_____

READ CHAPTER TWELVE

Chapter Twelve
The Power of Gold

The back garden of the Monastery of the Temple of the Twelve is a large circular garden. A circle of Golden Rain trees lines the outer periphery of the circular garden. The Golden Rain tree is so called as they produce abundant golden flowers in the spring and their leaves turn a mellow yellow-gold in the fall. This being the winter of the year, the trees are bare and look like skeletons with arms raised in supplication to the Colors. The inner ring of the garden is planted with flowers of a golden hue. The priests and priestesses of Gold love planting new species of flowers each season so there is always color surrounding the Chapel of Gold. A small walkway made of yellow bricks marks the way through the garden to the front door of the Chapel of Gold. As you walk down the yellow brick road and approach the front of the Chapel, a dazzling sight greets your eyes. Ornate gold carvings decorate the outside of the circular chapel building. The front door is a gleaming beacon of reflected light. It is a large door, twice the height of a person, and looks like it is made out of solid Gold. It is so beautiful it almost takes your breath away. You push on the door and it opens easily and silently. Odd, you say to yourself, that something as massive as this door should so easily open. As you walk inside the Chapel of Gold, the room glows with a soft golden light. Other than the soft golden light, the room appears rather plain. You find Caroline and Gawen seated at a plain, wooden table on rather plain, wooden chairs, waiting for you. A white table cloth with golden filigree covers the table. A large plate piled high with golden sweet cakes of every kind adorns the center of the table. Three golden goblets also are on top of the table.

"Greetings, dear reader," says Caroline as she rises out of her chair. She motions for you to sit in the chair opposite she and Gawen at the table. Gawen motions toward a priestess in a long, flowing, golden robe, and she brings a golden-amber-colored bottle to the table. He opens the bottle and pours some of the contents into the golden goblets.

"Share a toast to Gold with us," says Caroline as she raises her goblet. "To Gold. May his treasured light enhance and glorify all it shines upon."

You all touch goblets. You take a sip of the sparkling golden drink and find it both stimulating and refreshing. You find yourself relaxing in

Temple of the Twelve

the chair.

Caroline looks over at you and says, "Dear reader, have you in your life ever been gifted with a special treasure such as the small ring that belonged to Flight that Little Bird's mother gave her? Write down some thoughts of what that treasure meant to you then, and what it means to you now."

_____
_____
_____
_____
_____

"Little Bird was given a magic talisman - the three rings - the ring of her sister when young, the ring of her lover, and the armband of her grown sister." Caroline smiles and takes a sip from her golden goblet and then continues, "If you were to select a magic talisman to help you in your life's quest, share with us what it would be and how it would help you?"

_____
_____
_____
_____
_____

Gawen has a very thoughtful look on his face. Then he smiles at you and says, "Tara, novice of the Twelve, is struggling to confront and break free of a troubled and abusive past. Dear reader, are there things in your past that trouble you and that you wish to be free of? If you feel comfortable sharing them with us, write them down in the spaces below."

_____
_____
_____
_____
_____

Caroline looks at you with sadness in her eyes and says, "Little Bird has a vision of a past life when she served her people as one called Free Bird. Do you, dear reader, have memories of a past life that impacts your life in the here and now? What kind of past life was it; Gawen and I would very much like to know."

_____
_____
_____
_____
_____

Gawen leans back in his chair and looks at Caroline. She nods and smiles back at him. Gawen then looks at you and says, "Little Bird discovers the treasure of her heritage which fills the great emptiness that she felt inside. Dear reader, what is your heritage and what treasures does it hold for you?"

_____
_____
_____
_____
_____

Gawen says to you, "Gold has always been a symbol of wealth and prosperity. How do you define wealth? What does true wealth mean to you? Do you consider yourself blessed with the richness of Gold in your life?"

_____
_____
_____
_____

THE NATURE OF GOLD

From the dawn of time, man has been fascinated by gold. To the ancient alchemists, gold was called a noble metal because it does not oxidize under normal conditions. The ability of gold to retain its golden yellow color when other metals deteriorate over time made it the first choice for sacred jewelry and royal ornaments. Gold was easy for ancient man to obtain as it often occurs in its natural state, not requiring the smelting of ore as is the case with other metals. Gold, being malleable, was easy to work into whatever form was desired.

The tightly bound outer electron cloud of the gold atom brings about this seemingly divine characteristic of gold. Because the outer electrons in the gold atom are so tightly bound, they are not free to combine with other elements, such as oxygen. However, under the right conditions gold will combine with some other metals, such as silver and copper, forming alloys. Although these gold alloys have a slightly different color than pure gold, they all share the same "noble" characteristics as pure gold.

PRAYER TO GOLD

Thou color of royalty, of kings and princes, grant to me a sense of the value of my own self. Let me not esteem my own worth as too paltry and cheap. Teach me to walk through life conscious of my status as a beloved child of the Universe and ruler of my own life.

Thou color of wealth, of rich men and coins and jewelry, grant to me an understanding of true abundance. The Universe will give me all I need if I ask, but it does not happily grant those things I have not earned or which are not truly mine, or that I ask for out of greed. Grant to me a giving spirit, that I might offer my coat to the cold stranger in my path.

Thou great enhancer of beauty, which brings out the glory and majesty of jewels or paintings it frames, grant to me the ability to be for others a source of support. Teach me to accentuate, frame, decorate, or present the lives of others in settings that are worthy of them. May I always bring out the best in others, not overpowering but praising them.

Thou gold of autumn leaves and the glint of sunlight, yours is the power of radiance. You are pure and strong, and set a high standard. I strive to be worthy.

In all that I am, in all that I do, may I serve Gold.

OPTIONAL: Write Your Own Prayer to Gold:

_____
_____
_____
_____
_____
_____
_____
_____
_____
_____
_____
_____
_____
_____
_____
_____

JEWELRY FOR GOLD

Bless a special piece of gold jewelry, and dedicate it to Gold. When you wear it, remember you are in service to Gold. If you do not have gold jewelry, bless a special coin as your "good luck" coin, and ask Gold to bring you abundant prosperity and joy. As you wear your special piece of jewelry or carry your special coin, record your feelings and observations here.

_____
_____

Temple of the Twelve

_____
_____
_____
_____
_____
_____
_____
_____

Gawen says, "Congratulations, dear reader. Promise Gold that you will continue the quest for the hidden treasure of himself that is both within you and outside of you, and then locate the achievement page in the back of this journal and color one of the feather symbols gold."

Caroline smiles and says, "Dear reader, you are almost at the end of your quest with Little Bird. A fantastic adventure with Yellow awaits you in the next chapter. Gawen and I will meet you in the Gardens of Yellow on the Temple of the Twelve Monastery grounds after you have read Chapter Thirteen."

Gawen stands up from his chair and takes Caroline's hand as she also stands up from her chair. "May your journey with Yellow bring you great love and understanding," says Caroline as they both walk, hand in hand, out of the Chapel of Gold.

READ CHAPTER THIRTEEN

Chapter Thirteen
The Hope of Yellow

The gardens of Yellow are ablaze with color - a dizzying array of yellows and yellow-oranges - and in the center of the garden a small circular maze made of a neatly trimmed yellow flowering shrub. Mass plantings of yellow and yellow-orange Puff Flowers are arranged to form a large circle that encompasses the rest of the gardens. Puff Flowers are unique as spherical-shaped masses of petals and as the source for rare scented oils that fill the air around the gardens with a robust, sweet, musky aroma. Smaller plots in the inner gardens are planted with tall yellow and orange Ban Yan flowers that nod their large multi-petal flower heads in the slight afternoon breeze. The areas between the flower plots are covered with neatly manicured grass. The cool green is a powerful counterpoint to the intensity of the yellow flowers. At the very center of the garden is a small pond with a tinkling fountain. A school of yellow Azumi fish swims lazily in the dappled sunlight filtering through the water. Walking through these gardens, you can't help but feel warm and happy with a contentment born of complete trust. You find Caroline and Gawen sitting at a small table next to the pond. The table is covered with a bright yellow cloth, and there is a small bowl at the center of the table with yellow colored fruits inside. Three yellow glass chalices sit on the table. Each chalice is filled with a sparkling yellow liquid that looks remarkably like liquid sunshine. As you approach the table, Gawen rises and extends his hand in greeting.

"Greetings once again, dear reader," says Gawen as he motions for you to be seated at the table. You both sit down and Gawen continues, "Caroline and I are very interested in your thoughts on Little Bird's experience with Yellow."

Caroline takes a sip from her chalice, sits back in her chair, and says, "Little Bird's experience with Yellow is in essence all about trust. Put yourself in Little Bird's place. How would you react to Yellow's playfulness when she and Little Bird first meet?"

_____
_____
_____
_____
_____
_____

Temple of the Twelve

Gawen strokes his beard thoughtfully. "Hmmm, how, dear reader does your life compare with the level of trust that Little Bird experiences with Yellow? In what ways is it similar and/or different?"

_____
_____
_____
_____
_____
_____
_____

Caroline now looks at you with a very thoughtful expression, and asks, "Dear reader, can you think of ways that you in your own life can build a better trust bond with the Divine? Feel free to list these in the spaces below."

_____
_____
_____
_____
_____
_____
_____
_____

Gawen leans back in his chair and says, "Yellow tells Little Bird that she will complete the task set by Yellow without realizing it. Have you in your life experienced completing a task set for you by the Divine without realizing that you had completed that task until reflection afterward? Feel free to share your experience with us."

_____

Caroline sits forward in her chair with a very serious look on her face. She looks at you and says, "In this chapter Little Bird protects her friend Tara by stepping between Tara and the Dark Ones. Assume for a moment that you were in Little Bird's place. Given the constraints and background in your own life, how would you have reacted to this challenge?"

_____
_____
_____
_____
_____
_____
_____
_____

Gawen leans back in his chair, and with a serious look on his face, says, "Dear reader, has there been a time in your own life that you have felt like just giving up, much like Little Bird felt after protecting her friend, Tara? How did you recover from your own dark time?"

_____
_____
_____
_____
_____

Caroline, still with a serious look on her face, says, "Dear reader, it was the perfect love and trust of Yellow, of the Divine, and the memory of that trust and the love for her life mate that pulls Little Bird back from the brink of oblivion. Do you have this level of perfect love and trust with the Divine in your own life? In what ways do you think you could enhance and nourish that Divine trust in your own life?"

A VISUALIZATION AND AFFIRMATION FOR YELLOW

Sit for awhile in a quiet place where you will not be disturbed. Visualize yourself as you would be if you had perfect faith in the Divine's love of you. Yes, problems will come, but whatever challenges the Universe gives you will be challenges you can handle and will learn from. You will never be given a challenge that is pointless or will break your soul, and you believe that to the very core of you.

You live within that trust, planning for the future, but not spending your life in anxiety, fear and stress.

How does this visualization differ from you as you are now? What would your life be like if you lived in that kind of trust?

Every day for a month, say, "I live in perfect trust" before you get up for the day. How has this affected your life after doing it for a month?

PRAYER TO YELLOW

I open my life, my heart, my soul, to Yellow. I open myself to its exuberance and joy. I allow its brightness and cheerfulness to light up my dark corners. I dance in sunbeams and fields of sunflowers.

I open myself to optimism and hope. These things are not the gifts of foolish dreamers. Optimism and hope require strength.

Laughter shall echo in the halls of my home and the halls of my spirit. Laughter, music, kindness and gentleness shall be prominent in my life. The Universe sometimes provides hard lessons, but Yellow balances my life. It reminds me that love and happiness are real and possible and that the Universe is kind.

Behold, I am a child of the light because I have called myself so. I have chosen and claimed the brilliant Yellow light as my guide. Mine is the sunlight. Mine is the light of day.

Sweet Yellow, flow into me like honey, flow into me like streams of sunshine in my blood radiating out of me.

In all that I am, in all that I do, may I serve Yellow.

OPTIONAL: Write Your Own Prayer to Yellow:

Temple of the Twelve

_____
_____
_____
_____
_____
_____
_____
_____
_____
_____
_____
_____
_____
_____
_____
_____

Gawen smiles, leans back in his chair, and says, "Dear reader, in the story Tara is described as being destined to be a Warrioress of White. There are twelve groups, and each initiate must choose one of the twelve groups where they will have their primary service. Little Bird is in the Artist, group and Caroline and I are interested in where, if you were there in Little Bird's world, you would serve and why you would choose that group. We have provided a list of the twelve groups. You will see them listed along with their primary color below."

Caroline adds, "Remember you can be a priest or priestess of one color, in the service of another. For example, a priestess of Pink in the service of Black would be a compassionate, empathic healer who uses that gift in the areas of contemplation, prayer, and the occult. A priest of Brown in the service of Purple would be a man very connected to earth and nature. A man who loves working with his hands, but he would use that gift as a teacher. You can, for example, be a priest or priestess of Black in the service of Black – but for some, it is not that simple or clear cut.

Write down your choices in the spaces provided. After you have completed this task, locate the achievement page at the back of this journal and color a feather symbol yellow."

GROUPS OF THE TWELVE

Mystic/Contemplative/Historian/Record Keeper – BLACK

Artist/Musician/Writer/Visual Arts – RED

Warrior/Warrioress/Adventurer – GOLD

Judge/Mediator/Philosopher – WHITE

Scientist/Naturalist/Horticulturalist/Animal Husbandry/Cook/Craftsman – BROWN

Scholar/Educator/Teacher – PURPLE

Astronomer/Visionary/Psychic/Oracle/Messenger for the Temple of the Twelve – BLUE

Various Work/A focuser of hope and joy/Growth/Positive Thought/Light Bearer – YELLOW

Healer/Physician/Empath/Counselor – PINK

Treasurer of the Temple/Magician – SILVER

Can be in almost any type of service – indefinable, but if you feel it you serve it – ORANGE

Various Work/Focus on creativity and abundance in all fields – GREEN

Where would you serve?
_____
_____

Why?
_____
_____
_____
_____

Both Caroline and Gawen smile broadly at you and nod to each other as if some unspoken words have passed between them, then Caroline says, "Dear reader, you have almost completed your quest along with Little Bird. If you wish, take some time and re-visit the Hill of Novices and each of the color chapels. We will wait for you here. When you are ready, again if you wish, we will provide you with the Prayer to the Twelve. If you decide to recite the prayer, think about how you would arrange your own initiation if you were in Little Bird's world. The prayer to the Twelve is shown below".

PRAYER TO THE TWELVE COLORS

On the occasion of being recognized as a Priest/Priestess of the Twelve

On this most special day of my life, I, _____, call upon and invite the Twelve to be with me as I celebrate my crossing from the novitiate world to the world of full service to the Twelve as Priest or Priestess. I call upon the Twelve with a pure heart and the joy of all the challenges well met and completed.

I call upon Lady Black, she who has guided me to see and know myself. Lady Black, I hold in my hand the token that you bestowed upon me so long ago, and now place it lovingly as a part of the Circle of the Twelve. I pray that I shall never forget the lessons that you helped me to learn, and that I may be as a hollow reed through which you speak to those who seek your wisdom. Be with me now on this special day I pray, Lady Black.

I call upon Lord Brown, he who has been my teacher and guide as I have sought the love, beauty and truth that is all around me, and how to live in that love, beauty and truth. Lord Brown, may others be guided to beauty, truth and love by the example of my own life. Lord Brown, I hold in my hands the token that you gifted me with so long ago. I now place it lovingly as a part of the Circle of the Twelve. May I be a beacon to others to guide them to love, beauty and truth. Be with me now on this special day I pray, Lord Brown.

I call upon Lady White, she who has shown me that innocence is reborn within each of us as we show our love, care and compassion to those around us. Lady White, I pray that you will walk with me and be my guide as I help others to rebirth innocence in their own lives. May others who see my life perceive innocence reborn. Lady White, I hold in my hands the token that you bestowed upon me so long ago. I now place it lovingly as a part of the Circle of the Twelve. Be with me now on this special day I pray, Lady White.

I call upon Lord Silver, he who has gently shown me the magic that is within me, and how to harness that magic for the betterment of myself and the world. Lord Silver, I pray that you will continue to be my guide as I begin my service to the Twelve, that I may continue to nurture the magic within me so that I may help others find the magic within them. Lord Silver, I hold in my hand the token bestowed upon me so long ago, and now place it lovingly as a part of the Circle of the Twelve. Be with me now on this special day I pray, Lord Silver.

I call upon Lady Red, she who in her fiery way has taught me to seek courage, inspiration and strength. Lady Red, I pray that you will continue to be my guide as I begin my service to the Twelve, and to help others to seek you and your wisdom. May others see my life as an example of courage, inspiration and strength. Lady Red, I hold in my hands the token that you presented to me so long ago, and now I place it lovingly as a part of the Circle of the Twelve. Be with me now on this special day I pray, Lady Red.

I call upon Lord Orange, he who has been my friend and guide in learning how to be one with the Divine force. Lord Orange, I pray that you will always be my friend and guide as I begin my service to the twelve, and to teach others how to know the Divine force as friend. I pray that others may know that the Divine is their friend by looking at my life. Lord Orange, I hold in my hands the token that you gifted to me so long ago, and that I now place lovingly as a part of the Circle of the Twelve. Be with me now on this special day I pray, Lord Orange.

I call upon Lady Green, she who has helped

me to know my greatest pleasures and to open to them, so that I can achieve my greatest destiny. I pray that I will always be open to my greatest pleasures, and that as I begin my service to the Twelve, my life will serve as guiding light to those who have need of it. Lady Green, I pray that you always walk with me as I begin this new adventure. Lady Green, I hold in my hands that token you gave to me so long ago, and that I now lovingly place as a part of the Circle of the Twelve. Be with me now on this special day I pray, Lady Green.

I call upon Lord Blue, he who has guided me to understand that the Divine lives through us and to see the world through his eyes. I pray that the Divine will always live within me and I within the Divine spirit. May my life serve as a guidepost to those who seek the Divine as I begin my service to the Twelve. Lord Blue, I pray that you will always be within me as I will always be within you as I begin this new chapter in my life. Lord Blue, I hold in my hands the token you bestowed upon me so long ago, and that I now lovingly place as a part of the Circle of the Twelve. Be with me now on this special day I pray, Lord Blue.

I call upon Lady Yellow, she who has been my guide in discovering perfect trust and love. I pray that I shall always trust in the Twelve and in Yellow. May my life be a guide for those seeking perfect trust and love in their own lives as I begin my service to the Twelve. Lady Yellow, I pray that you will be with me as my guide as I walk into this new adventure in my life. Lady Yellow, I hold in my hands the token you presented to me so long ago, and that I now lovingly place as a part of the Circle of the Twelve. Be with me now on this special day I pray, Lady Yellow.

I call upon Lord Gold, he who has guided me to find the treasures in my life. I pray, Lord Gold, that you and your loving radiance shall always be with me as I seek those treasures in my life that yet lie undiscovered. May those who I encounter as I serve the Twelve see through my life the treasures in their own lives and know you, Lord Gold. My Lord, I hold in my hands the token you gave to me so long ago, and now lovingly place it as a part of the Circle of the Twelve. Be with me now on this special day I pray, Lord Gold.

I call upon Lady Pink, she who has helped me heal my three greatest heart wounds. I pray, Lady Pink, that you will always be with me as I begin my service to the Twelve. Through my life of service to the Twelve, may others who are hurting find healing of their own heart wounds. Lady Pink, I hold in my hands the token you gifted to me so very long ago, and now I lovingly place it as a part of the Circle of the Twelve. Be with me now on this special day I pray, Lady Pink.

I call upon Lord Purple, he who guided me to a healing of my three greatest spiritual wounds and who showed me the love and joy of learning. I pray, Lord Purple, that as I begin this service with the Twelve, that you will be with me. May my life be a beacon of hope to those who are hurting spiritually, and through me may they be healed. Lord Purple, I hold in my hands the token you bestowed on me so long ago, and that I now lovingly place as a part of the Circle of Twelve. Be with me now on this special day I pray, Lord Purple.

As I gaze upon these tokens of the Circle of the Twelve, I pray that I will be the priest/priestess I was born to be. May this circle of color surround and fill me with love, care, compassion, and a spiritual fire that burns deep within my soul. I pray that all the Twelve will walk with me as I walk with them, as I step forward into this next chapter in my life, and may:

The depth of Black,

the security of Brown,

the power of Gold,

the hope of Yellow,

the wisdom of Blue,

the life of Green,

the sacredness of Purple,

the caring of Pink,

the glory of Orange,

the passion of Red,

the magic of Silver,

the rebirth of White,

Be with me always.

Blessed be the Circle of the Twelve, and blessed am I who reside in its center.

###

If you wish, describe how you see your own initiation as a Priest or Priestess of the Twelve.

_____
_____
_____
_____
_____
_____
_____
_____
_____
_____
_____
_____
_____
_____
_____
_____
_____
_____
_____
_____
_____
_____

Gawen and Caroline rise from their seats, extend their hands to you, and say in unison, "Dear reader, it has been a pleasure walking with you on this fantastic quest through the colors. We would like to congratulate you on a journey well-taken and wish you well on your future adventures. May the colors of the Twelve be with you always. Blessed be, dear reader, and farewell."

Gawen and Caroline walk slowly, arm in arm, through the gardens of Yellow.

BLESSED BE THE CIRCLE OF THE TWELVE.

BLESSED BE YOU WHO RESIDE AT ITS CENTER.

Temple of the Twelve

Section Two
Using this Journal with Children

CHAPTER ONE – BLACK

If you prefer not to use a candle, get some Play-Doh®. Have your child create something that represents what they are afraid of or want to change in their life. They can write a word in the Play-Doh®, or make a figure (for example, a child scared of big dogs can make a dog.) Then have the child squish this clay back into a ball. Have them make something to take the place of the "bad thing" they just made (for example, a child struggling with divorce can make three figures that represent him and his parents, each holding his hand to represent that both parents are still his allies.)

Explain to the child that the Play-Doh® is like their life. They can make something good or bad out of the same clay, it's their choice.

CHAPTER TWO – PINK

When doing the Month of Kindness project, make a big chart for your child with stickers, gold stars, and so on. Record the things the child has done that day on the chart. Do things with the child, (for example, if a child has a parent who is a firefighter, make cookies for the firehouse and deliver them with the child as a thank you.)

CHAPTER THREE – SILVER

Have your child write a short story, draw a picture, or best yet, put on a simple play about magic. It can be about faeries, elves, witches, wizards, aliens with super powers, whatever draws the child. Get three books from the library or bookstore about your child's chosen theme (for example, if he writes about pirates and mermaids, get three books about those.) Choose well-written, classic stories, and read them with your child.

CHAPTER FOUR – BLUE

For a week or a month, find all the blue things you can with your child. Eyes, sky, birds, stones, clothes, berries, water, anything and everything blue you can find. Make a list and see what the child thinks about the color blue after making the list. Perhaps make it a contest to see who comes up with the bluest things. Another idea is an adventure on the water, be it a lake or ocean, or a hot air balloon ride where you see the blue sky spread out - anything that expresses the immensity of blue. Another option, if they are in season, is to take your child blueberry picking.

One last idea - challenge your child to do a search on the computer and find twenty interesting quotes about the color blue. Have them record all twenty, and see how he feels about blue after reading the twenty quotes from others.

CHAPTERS FIVE – SIX AND SEVEN - RED AND GREEN

RED

Get some red construction paper and make a collage of red paper hearts. On each, have your child draw a picture (they can cut it from a magazine, draw it themselves, or just write words, or use actual photographs) of something they love.

Hang the hearts up somewhere where the child will always see them, to remember the things that mean the most to them. You can make the hearts into a mobile by punching a hole in each heart and stringing them up, or you can use a piece of poster board as a collage. You can hang them on the refrigerator, or use them as bookmarks - whatever works best for your child, wherever they will see it often. If your child does not want hearts, or if your child seems too "old" for such a collage (though even adults can enjoy them!) just use a red piece of poster board or red markers. The point is to surround the things they love with the passionate, bright color. A red photo album or scrapbook would also work. Or a red frame that you can put photos in.

GREEN

Adopt a plant or tree. You can buy one, anything from a small potted plant to a little tree the child can watch grow huge over the years. Or you can just pick one from a neighboring park. Have the child research what it is that this particular plant or tree needs to survive. Have them research the characteristics of the plant or tree. You can do fun things like give the plant or tree a name, hang ribbons or ornaments on the branches, decorate it for holidays. Take photographs of the plant or tree in different seasons or stages of growth.

Tell the child it is their responsibility to care for, feed and water the tree or plant, and show them how to do so. If it is something that gives flowers, bring some of the flowers to a nearby nursing home. If it is a vegetable, teach the child how to cook the vegetable they grew. If it is a tree, all sorts of decorations can be made from pinecones, acorns, or autumn leaves. If you live in a place where you can get a coconut tree, harvest coconuts. If you live in a place where all you can have is a small green plant on a shelf, do that.

Of course if your family has a large garden, or berry or tree farm, that opens up opportunities as well. The important thing here is to have the child form a relationship with the plant or tree. They should learn to care about it. You know your child. If they want to build a tree house in "their" tree, help them do it. If they want a swing in "their" tree, help them build one. If there is a willow at a nearby park that they love, use that. If they love tomatoes, grow a tomato plant.

Here is a wonderful example of how to teach your child of the love and power within the green of growing plants and trees. About ten years ago, for the children's section of a music festival, two hundred sunflowers were planted by the children who then sang this song written by Yvette Benedict;

INTO THE GARDEN

First Verse

Plants and weeds, rocks and seeds, the sun is shining bright

I'm a flower. I can bend as long as my roots hold tight.

Chorus

I'm a flower, face the sun, water rains on everyone.

In this garden life is good, it's a growing neighborhood.

Be a flower, share the sight of color, shape, reflect the light.

Clouds may come, but when they go, the water has helped me grow.

These are the planting instructions for the sunflowers:

1. Pick a sunny spot where no one will step on me.

2. Dig a hole, one foot by one foot. (The size of two shoe boxes)

3. Take all grass and weeds out of the newly dug soil.

4. Place a peat pot so its top is level with the ground.

5. Water me a little every day; please don't let me dry out.

6. Wait, and with a little patience, I'll be a beautiful Sunflower. Watch how my flower face follows the path of the sun every day.

7. When I hang my head and don't look at the sun anymore, I'm ready to be eaten. If you don't want my seeds, your feathered friends do!

Thank You!

the Sunflower

Use your knowledge of the child to help pick the right tree or plant.

If you want to attract birds or butterflies or squirrels to your tree or plant, research how to do so. Buy a bird feeder. Make this a real and loving relationship between the child and the tree or plant - one that lasts, and grows.

CHAPTER EIGHT – ORANGE

Have an "Orange Party." This can be as simple or elaborate as you wish, with two people or dozens of your child's friends. Get into the celebratory, joyous, life-affirming nature of orange. Make all the guests wear something orange. Buy orange party hats, balloons, streamers, paper plates and napkins, as much orange as you can find. Find tiny orange "fairy lights", get orange flowers. Have a bowl of oranges on the table. Have cookies or cupcakes with orange frosting. Light orange candles on a cake.

There can be a lot of themes for the Orange Party. You can have each guest bring a gift for a needy child that you later donate. You can have a movie marathon. You can have a clown or a magician. You can have a bonfire (lots of orange flames) and roast marshmallows. Have your daughter and her friends paint their toe nails orange. Buy orange wigs. You can make it a working party, and paint a mural in a play room. The ideas are limited only by your imagination ... orange likes to play.

If your child likes to knit or crochet, make orange slippers or a scarf at the party. If they like to cook, make a carrot cake or an orange gelatin salad with them. Get a candle making kit and make orange candles. Get a jewelry making kit and make orange bracelets. Paint orange racing stripes on your child's toy car. Do face painting with orange flowers, lightning bolts, or suns. Get a big bag of orange cheddar popcorn and feed some of it to the kids and some to the birds. Buy six orange hula hoops and have a hula hoop party. If your child dances or sings, have them put on a performance wearing an orange costume. Put temporary orange streaks in your child's hair if you are a hairdresser or know a lot about it, have a "waiting for the Great Pumpkin" party if it's Halloween. Gather orange leaves if it is autumn. Buy an orange fish and have a "welcome to the family" party for the fish. The party should fit the nature of the child or children it is for.

Don't let money block your creativity, either. With very little money you can still have a pumpkin carving party with you and your child if it's Halloween, or draw pictures with orange crayons with your toddler. Again, this can be a very simple party - or not.

What needs to get expressed here is the connection between orange and laughter, joy, health, happiness, warmth, vitality, and fun. It will be even more meaningful if you try to add some kindness to it - take six orange flowers or orange balloons to a patient in a hospital. Do something good at the party – for example, decorate a rocking chair by painting orange flowers on it for the old lady down the street who has no money. The child should leave the party with this understanding - orange helps provide the capacity for exuberance and real appreciation of life.

CHAPTER NINE – PURPLE

This should be a fun and enlightening exercise for you and your child. Inform them that they are "Teacher for a Day". They are to prepare a half hour class with YOU as the student.

The topic should be something the child is very interested in, whether that is cars, computers, music, math, current events and so on. Give the teacher as much time as you think they need to prepare the class, but it's unlikely they will need more than a couple of weeks. Offer help if the teacher needs supplies or getting things copied or printed. Help set up the classroom with desks and chairs (even if it's just a card table.)

You can set up a "What did I Learn Today" chart. Here the child is encouraged to write a sentence, or even a few words, about something interesting to them that they learned that day, and post it on the chart. You can use gold stars or stickers on the chart as rewards for particularly inspiring postings. You can make a new chart each month, saving the old charts. Later, you and your child can go back and look at all the learning that has taken place over the previous months.

Purple represents enlightenment, knowledge, understanding, deep spiritual connection, and a reverence for all things holy. In this class, seek to have your child feel a reverence for knowledge. Instill in them that learning is fun as well as hard work.

And yes - the teacher can give homework.

CHAPTER TEN – BROWN

Help your child build a collection of rocks, crystals, minerals, and semiprecious gemstones. If money is a concern, collect interesting rocks and pretty stones anywhere you see them. If you have discretionary money to spend, visit a local gem and mineral show or a new age store to obtain samples for the collection. The collection can be as small as a few stones in a pretty dish or bowl, or as large as you wish, depending on the child's level of interest.

Some tips:

1. Encourage the child to participate in the collecting.

2. Obtain a Field Guide for rocks and minerals and help your child identify each sample as it is collected. Make sure to label each sample with a number and name of the rock or mineral.

3. Have your child keep a notebook where they can write down information about each sample in their collection.

4. As you travel, point out the different landforms you encounter and discuss with your child how these landforms were created and how weathering changes them over time.

5. Allow your child to begin to appreciate the wonder of the earth we walk on but so often do not see or understand.

CHAPTER ELEVEN – WHITE

White is the color of goodness and purity. It is often hard for us, adult or child, to really see the good and beauty in ourselves. Make a "What is Beautiful about Me" or a "What is Great about Me" chart. This can be added to with photographs or drawings if the child wishes, which show the good things about the child.

Have the child write ten things that make him good, beautiful, special, and unique. Put it in a place where they can always see it. If you want to make it more elaborate, have people the child loves and respects write something on the chart about the child. Make an "autograph" section on the chart. This way the child can always see the words their heroes and heroines wrote about them.

Another idea: If the chart seems boring, try a "What's Great about Me" tee-shirt the child paints themselves, or with friends and family. There are also trophies and medals available that you can personalize. Or there are stuffed animals into which you can record a special message about the wonderfulness of the child. The child can play it back whenever they want. On that theme, you can video tape or audiotape people saying what is wonderful about the child, for the child to keep. Do whatever makes the child feel how incredible he or she is.

CHAPTER TWELVE – GOLD

Give the child some money - $1, $5, $10, $100, it doesn't matter, whatever fits your budget. Tell your child to think of ways that they can do as much as possible for someone else with that money. In what ways can they spread it around? Can they find ways to multiply their money and give more?

Tell the child to ask everyone they help to do something good for someone else, and thus ripple out the giving even more. See if parents will do this with your child's friends, and make it a group activity for them. Explain to the child that wealth and abundance return tenfold to you when you share.

CHAPTER THIRTEEN – YELLOW

Yellow is such a loving color, so warm and giving, so full of joy and good, healthy laughter. In thinking of yellow, not one but several images come to mind. Pick any of these ideas that might suit your child:

1. If you are open to and looking at having a pet, get a yellow bird, a "yellowish" cat, or golden retriever if you are looking for a larger pet, or even a yellow fish. The connection between the joy of yellow and having to take CARE of something is a good one, because yellow is about nurturing.

2. Find a yellow teddy bear and tell your child to hug it (or think of it) when they need a smile.

3. Plant sunflowers or other yellow flowers - yellow roses, tulips, daffodils, marigolds. Take a photo of your child with all the sunshiny yellow flowers and frame it for them.

4. Get yellow construction paper, and have the child create ten or twenty smiley faces, with the message, "Just wanted to bring you a smile today". Have them give the smiley faces to people - friends, or even strangers if you are with them while they do it.

Alternately, get ten to twenty yellow balloons and pass them out with a message on them, "Have a bright, happy day." Or pass out yellow cupcakes with yellow frosting to some people who would really enjoy them.

5. Get a butterfly raising kit, with butterflies that will have some yellow in them, and help the child raise and set free the butterflies.

6. Get a yellow kite and fly it, maybe at a park or the beach with a picnic.

7. If you are open to your child lighting candles, get a dozen yellow candles and have your child light them, making a wish, prayer, or affirmation as they light each one.

8. Find your child a fun yellow hat, or yellow sneakers. Alternately, knit or crochet a yellow hat and scarf, slippers, or sweaters.

9. Have your child write a report on sunlight, and why it appears yellow, and why it is warm. Why do people need sunlight to live? What is the effect of people when they have less sunlight in the winter? Another idea is to write a report on why there are yellow, red, white and blue stars. Alternately, have them write a report about why bananas, corn, yellow squash, honey, cheese, or yellow apples are good and healthy to eat. Or write a report on how butter or honey is made. And you can make a meal with some of these foods after the child writes the report(s).

Temple of the Twelve

Experiential Journal

Self Portrait at the End of My Journey

Temple of the Twelve

Experiential Journal

Temple of the Twelve
Achievement Chart

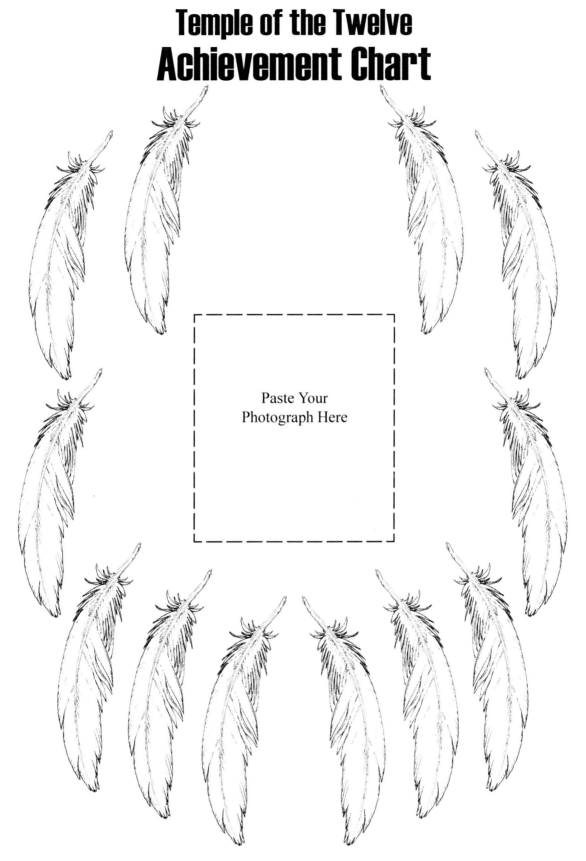

After you complete each chapter in the Experiential Journal,
color-in a feather the appropriate color for the chapter

Temple of the Twelve

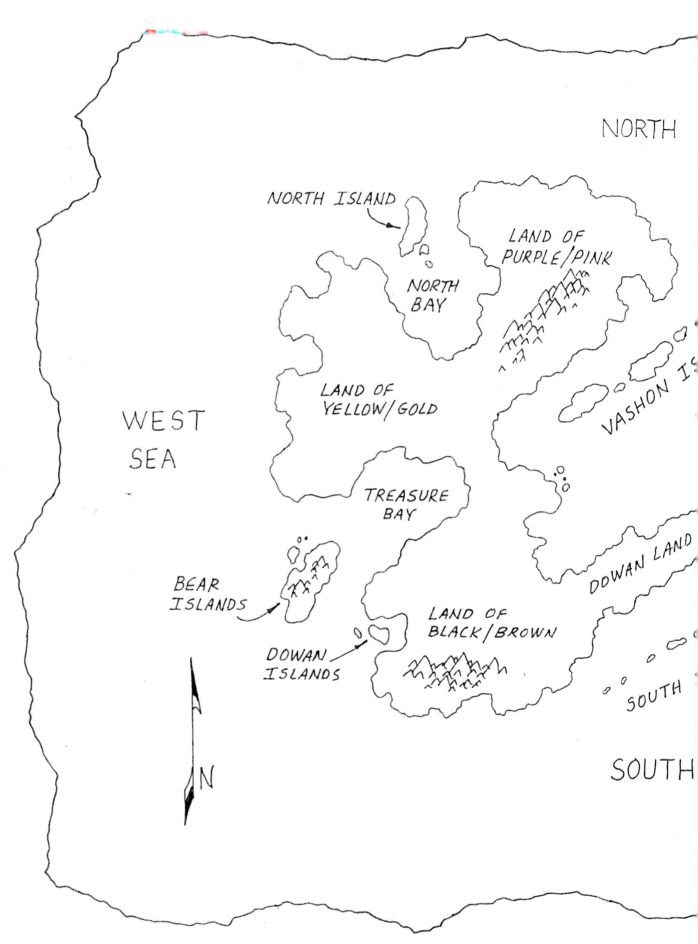

Experiential Journal

The Authors

Esmerelda Little Flame lives in Connecticut, in the same old white house where her father was born and teaches piano at the music studio her parents built in the early fifties.

She is an avid tarot reader with a special talent for creating guided story journeys from the readings. Other passions include drumming, scrying, rune reading, creating ritual, working with the faeries, the study of theatre, and the study of empathy and human connection.

Esmerelda holds Baccalaureate degrees in English and Social Work with a Masters degree in Pastoral Counseling.

Her first book was *The Adventures of Charles the Well-Traveled Bear.*

Dr. David Babulski is the author of over sixty technical publications in the disciplines of physics, electronics, aeronautics, mineralogy and astronomy. He holds a Baccalaureate degree in Earth Science and Masters and Doctoral degrees in Science Education. He also holds a diploma from the Institute for Children's Literature and he is an award winning mineral artist. Professionally he is a technical educator with over thirty-four years of experience.

In his spare time, he is writing several books, plays the Celtic harp and is active in model aeronautics, mineral art, amateur radio, astronomy and is a student of metaphysics.

Other Books Available from Andborough Publishing

ISBN : 978-0-9774181-5-2
paperback

Only $17.95

Children's Reiki Handbook, 2nd Edition

Reiki is an Japanese system of energy healing through the "laying on of hands" that is simple enough for children of all ages to learn.

The Children's Reiki Handbook is a guide to energy healing that provides kids with the information they need to prepare for their First, Second and Master Reiki Attunement; and shows them how to use their new skills to heal themselves and others.

"I found Children's Reiki Handbook to be a concise yet thorough introduction to the Usui healing system of Reiki. It's perfect for children and young adults"
- ML Rhodes, Amazon #1 Best Selling Author and Usui Reiki Ryoho Master/Teacher

"If you want to learn Reiki, this book will serve as in inspiration towards that goal... This Reiki handbook is a great resource to introduce the benefits of Reiki healing to children or grown ups who are just starting out."
-Erin Kelly-Allshouse, Review Editor
Children of the New Earth

Voices of Our Mountain Kin, Volume 1

Voices of Our Mountain Kin is a collection of legends, folk tales and memories of our heritage set in the Blue Ridge, Balsam and Great Smoky Mountains. You'll enjoy wonderful old-time stories of mountain medicines and healing, moon-shining, ghosts, superstitions and faith, Civil War tragedies, pioneer living, love stories and much more

$17.95

ISBN-13: 978-0-9774181-2-1
ISBN-10: 0-9774181-2-X
143 pages paperback

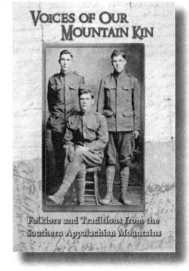

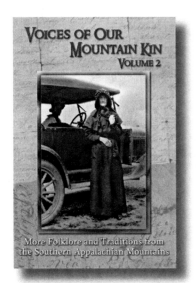

Voices of Our Mountain Kin, Volume 2

Volume 2 of Voices of Our Mountain Kin, continues with more of the legends, folk tales and memories of our heritage in the Blue Ridge, Balsam and Great Smoky Mountains that you enjoyed reading in the first volume.

You'll experience the hardships of pioneer living and the struggle to survive and prosper in the early days of the Southern Appalachia. Family stories will lead you through clearing virgin forest and breaking ground for the first homesteads, impacts of the Civil War, mountain medicines, midwives and healing, to more recent, modern times.

ISBN-13: 978-0-9774181-6-9
ISBN-10: 0-9774181-6-2
164 pages paperback

$17.95

Temple of the Twelve, Volume 1: Novice of Colors

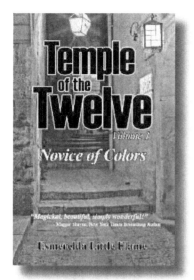

The sixteen year old daughter of a poor woodcutter, Caroline was born into a world where the Twelve were said to be the stuff of legends and children's stories.

She had always known the truth – that the Twelve were very real and living amongst humankind even now. But when she ended up at their Temple she didn't quite believe it was real herself.

Still, when the Twelve began to appear to her in human form – when they began to teach her their lessons – they changed everything in her life. She began to understand that it was her destiny to be a bridge between the past and the future in a world that was changing too fast.

She formed bonds with an ancient clan who kept the ways of the Twelve alive, in hiding and seclusion. Her love for the Twelve deepened into unconditional loving devotion – It was a love that would take her from girlhood into the soul of a young woman.

For love of the Twelve, Caroline began to understand, she would do anything...Anything at all.

ISBN-13: 978-0-9774181-8-3
278 pages paperback

$17.95

"Magickal, beautiful, simply wonderful!"
- Maggie Shayne, New York Times Bestselling Author

"...prose is music to the mind...weaves a whimsical tapestry of warmth and delight..."
- Silver Ravenwolf, Bestselling Author of *Teen Witch* and *Solitary Witch*

Dream of the Circle of Women

Soon after arriving at the house she's just inherited from the birth mother she never met, Kat begins to have a series of vivid recurring dreams about a group of women who drown themselves in the sea rather than be persecuted as witches.

As she learns about her new home and her birth mother, Kat finds herself with more and more questions, discovers hidden secrets in the centuries old house, and uncovers a disturbing truth of her lineage. But will she find the answers she needs before tragedy strikes her?

ISBN-13: 978-0-9774181-9-0
330 pages paperback

$17.95

What others are saying about
Dream of the Circle of Women...

"...Blanchard manages to completely enrapture the reader...Dream [of the Circle of Women] is a masterpiece for readers of any age group. Well done, and more...please!"
– Shelley Glodowski, Senior Reviewer Midwest Book Review

"This is by far one of the best pagan fiction books I have found. Dream of the Circle of Women is imaginative, engaging, and inspiring."
– Jennifer Erwin, Facing North Book Reviews